Bed, Breakfast & Bike
Midwest

by

Robert & Theresa Russell

Bed, Breakfast & Bike Midwest
Copyright 2000 by Robert & Theresa Russell

Cover: *photos by Robert & Theresa Russell, design by Jean Sullivan*

Maps: *Richard Widhu*

ISBN: 0-933855-17-6
Library of Congress Control Number: 00-135824

Also available:
Bed, Breakfast & Bike Northeast
Bed, Breakfast & Bike Pacific Northwest
Bed, Breakfast & Bike Western Great Lakes
RIDE GUIDE: Covered Bridges of Ohio
RIDE GUIDE: North Jersey 2nd Edition
RIDE GUIDE: Central Jersey 2nd Edition
RIDE GUIDE: South Jersey 2nd Edition
RIDE GUIDE: New Jersey Mountain Biking
RIDE GUIDE: Mountain Biking in the New York Metro Area
RIDE GUIDE: Hudson Valley New Paltz to Staten Island 2nd Edition
and
Happy Endings by Margaret Logan

Send for our catalog or visit us at <u>www.anacus.com</u>

Published by

PRESS INC.

P.O. Box 156, Liberty Corner, New Jersey 07938

"Ride Guide" and "Bed, Breakfast and Bike" are trademarks of Anacus Press, Inc.

Printed in the United States of America

For Gram

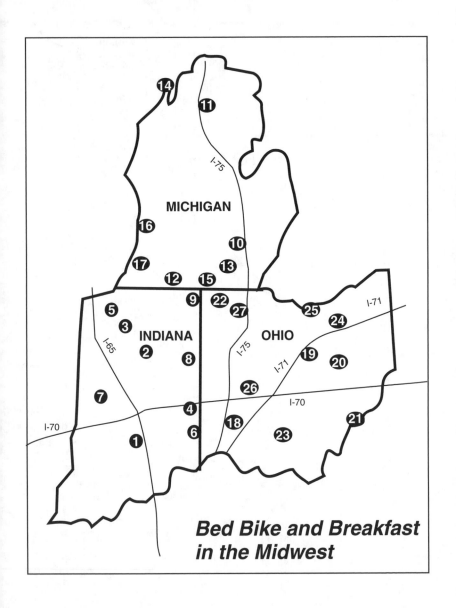

Bed Bike and Breakfast in the Midwest

Contents

Acknowledgments

Special thanks to the innkeepers for hosting us and providing us with information on local attractions, suggestions for scenic cycling routes, or referrals to local cyclists. Without their help and hospitality, this book wouldn't exist.

To Carol Rider for filling in and assisting as needed.

To our children—Erik, Tatiana, Jeff, and Nathan—for holding down the fort in our absence.

To our editor, Christian Glazar who patiently stood by us in spite of a bout with a kidney stone, family death, house fire, and other incidents that delayed our research.

To local tourism directors who promoted their regions as biking destinations and offered their assistance in route development and chosing bed and breakfasts. Thanks to all of you.

Preface

Pedaling at a leisurely pace, you become attuned to your surroundings. Your senses are heightened as you keenly observe your environment—the smell of pine trees, the sounds of the forest, the visual beauty around you, the feel of the earth beneath your wheels, and—perhaps the ultimate reason for cycling—the taste of regional cuisine. On a bike you notice things that are mere blurs from the window of an automobile. Biking transcends generations; senior citizens, children, and everyone in between can enjoy this pastime.

At the end of a day of cycling and exploring, a pleasant stay in a bed and breakfast enhances the total experience. What better way to form a lasting impression of a region? Both give you the opportunity to experience first hand the best a particular location has to offer. Bicycling provides just the right pace to sense your surroundings. Lodging at an inn allows you to experience an area on a more personal and intimate level than a stay in a generic motel room just off the highway. The ambiance, architecture, or history of your accommodations will make your stay memorable, and you'll have the added advantage of an attentive host who's eager to share a wealth of information about the area.

We have chosen the establishments and locations in this book because they offer plenty to keep you occupied. You certainly don't have to be a cyclist to participate; non-cycling companions will find a variety of attractions to keep them entertained. Whatever your interests may be, you are sure to find several destinations to suit you. Our goal for this book is simply to suggest some great inns and to lead you to the nearby points of interest and scenery that make these destinations so wonderful.

We hope you enjoy the bed and breakfasts and the biking as much as we did.

How To Use This Book

Information About the B&Bs

We have purposely selected a wide variety of inns; each has a unique ambiance, architecture, or décor, combining to give you a memorable experience. Most of the inns are located in rural or small town locations, ideal for bicycling in low-traffic areas. Your inn could be a Queen Anne Victorian, full of antiques; an Amish-style farmhouse, with its simple and practical furnishings; a converted mill; a castle in the country, or just about anything you could imagine.

We have included a broad variety of price ranges, as well. Because rates fluctuate fairly often, we have given a price category instead of an actual dollar amount. The theory: Five years down the road, an inn that is moderately priced will probably still be moderately priced. On the other hand, $100 will buy you a moderate room in 2000, but perhaps only a budget room in 2005. For the sake of comparison, we used the ranges below as a rough guide at press time:

> **Budget:** $90 or less
> **Moderate:** $91-140
> **Deluxe:** $141-199
> **Luxury:** $200 and up

You may wish to consider a midweek or off-season visit, when the innkeepers often offer lower rates.

The book is divided into sections by state with sections at the end for recipes and information sources. Each section starts with a brief introduction to bicycling in that particular state.

Each inn has its own chapter. In the heading lists the essential information for contacting the inn, including the address, phone and fax numbers, e-mail and web addresses where applicable, name of the innkeepers, and rate range.

Following this information is an in-depth look at the accommodations, the area where the inn is located, and attractions and points of interest.

Cycling

The **Biking from the Inn** section is broken down into the following self-explanatory components:

> **Terrain**
> **Traffic**
> **Road Conditions**
> **Nearest Bike Shop**
> **Mountain Biking Opportunities** (where applicable)

To create the cycling routes from each inn, we gathered a lot of information from local cycling clubs, tourism bureaus, and state bicycling coordinators. Others we developed ourselves. Some routes may be official cycling routes with signs provided by the state or county, and others use the routes of organized rides and have arrows painted on the roads. We have tried to combine rail-trail riding as an option, especially in areas that might otherwise have challenging terrain. We've included a variety of distances, and most of the routes can easily be shortened or lengthened.

You'll see the best the Midwest has to offer on these routes: historic towns and buildings, rivers, lakes, forests, covered bridges, canals, farms, and barns. Don't automatically assume that a flat ride will be easy—we have something called wind that often makes up for the lack of hills. You might want to consider reversing a route to come back with a tailwind if the wind is a major factor on the day you travel.

We researched these routes carefully—sometimes with many backtracking expeditions—just so that you could have a carefree ride, without having to turn around and re-pedal miles of road to find your way. If you ride with others with computers, you know that everybody doesn't always come out with the exact same mileage at the end of the same route. We used a few different computers, because one died after 10,000 miles—though not without a few sporadic attempts to carry on. The replacement calculated in hundredths, which posed a dilemma—do we round up or down? In any case, there should be no more than 1/10 of a mile discrepancy between your computer and the cue sheet. If you *do* find any major errors in the route descriptions or cue sheets, please write and let us know.

To follow the **cue sheets**, use the following legend:

Cum.	- Cumulative mileage from starting point
Street/	- Descriptions of street names and
Landmark	distinguishing landmarks
Dir.	- Direction
R	- Right turn
L	- Left turn
BR	- Bear right
BL	- Bear left
SL	- Sharp left
SR	- Sharp right
S	- Straight
-	- Point of interest
TA	- Turn around

Maps

Use the maps in this book in conjunction with a good county map. This is especially necessary if you decide to alter a route or follow road signs to another destination. As a side note, we found many maps highly inaccurate, so if you do divert from our routes, it's always a good idea to ask the locals whenever there is a question about directions.

The Cole House in Peru, Indiana, was built by J.O. Cole, the grandfather of composer and lyricist Cole Porter (see page 27).

Before You Go

Choosing your destination
We thoroughly enjoyed each and every destination we visited. A few things should be taken into consideration when selecting your destination. The following is to help you make a good choice.

How much time do I have?
While we suggest at least two nights at a particular destination, not every person has that luxury of time. If, for example, you only have one night and two days to spare, consider how much time you will spend driving. Driving several hours is fatiguing and then cycling an additional several hours can be exhausting. Perhaps an inn within 2-3 hours of home would be ideal for a short and pleasant visit. On the other hand, an inn located just up the road can seem like it's miles away from your daily grind. We found some of the inns that are very close to home just as restful and exciting as those far away—we didn't even think about how close we were to home.

What restrictions does the inn have?
All prohibit inside smoking. Some don't allow alcohol, which could be a consideration if you are planning a celebration. Some don't allow children.

Am I allergic to or uncomfortable with animals?
Check to see if there are resident pets.

How large is the inn?
If you are planning on going with your local cycling group, be sure the number of rooms and the sleeping arrangements work. If you want to have a relatively quiet or private stay, choose a small inn or one with a suite or detached unit. If, on the other hand, you are a social animal, choose a larger inn.

Do I get up during the night?
Private baths may be more to your liking.

How close do I want to be to the action?
If you want to be able to walk to restaurants, shops, and other forms of entertainment, an in-town location is good for you. If you want to see the stars, birdwatch, or just get away from it all, a country location may suit you.

What interests me?
See what types of attractions are in the area. If antiques and shopping interest you, there are plenty of destinations in this book. Or maybe you want to check out the Amish lifestyle, or ride over covered bridges, or do all your riding within sight of water. Each area has its own unique appeal.

What suits my taste?
Read the descriptions and see what matches your preferences. Request a certain room if it appeals to you; likewise, avoid a certain room if it is not your taste. You want to feel comfortable in your surroundings.

What is my fitness level and riding ability?
If you are in shape and ride often you should be able to handle any of the routes. If you aren't, consider your fitness level and chose a route with gentle terrain. A short, flat ride or a rail-trail might be a better choice than a long, hilly route.

These are just a few questions to consider. Contact the innkeepers and ask questions; they are glad to help you and want your inn experience to match your needs. Check out web pages or request brochures. These often have photos of the rooms and the inn itself.

Preparation
Training and maintaining a comfortable level of physical fitness will definitely contribute to your enjoyment of these bicycling routes. However, many of the routes encourage you to stop, take plenty of time for exploration, and have low mileage options. Riding your bicycle for just an hour a day will improve your muscle shape and get you comfortable on your seat.

Your bicycle should also be in good shape. Tune it up yourself or have it done at a local bike shop. Be sure you know how to do simple repairs such as fixing a flat, adjusting your seat, or putting the chain back on the cogs.

For day trips, the following items are suggested (a rack trunk or handlebar bag are good options for carrying these things):

> **Air pump**
> **Spare tube**
> **Patch kit**
> **First aid kit**
> **Water**
> **Snacks**
> **Sunscreen**
> **Rain jacket for rain or warmth**
> **Cell phone or change for phone call**
> **Lock and cable**

Of course, a helmet is strongly recommended, as are cycling gloves. A computer for measuring distance is especially helpful when road signs are missing or when following cue sheets.

Become familiar with the cycling laws of the state in which you are traveling and keep in mind some basic safety recommendations: ride with traffic, signal turns, and follow all traffic laws.

—Important Disclaimer—

While this book provides as accurate a description of these rides as possible, road conditions and other critical information provided in these pages can change overnight. It is your own responsibility to have a thorough understanding of the routes you ride, the mechanical condition of your bike, and your riding ability. By purchasing this book or borrowing it from a friend, you have released Anacus Press, the authors, and the artists from any liability for injuries you may sustain while using this book as a guide.

Bicycling the Midwest

For many, the word "Midwest" brings to mind images of endless cornfields. That image is partly true, because this is the heartland after all. You will see plenty of farms, but you may also be pleasantly surprised—if not in awe—of the diverse topography and impressive scenery found in this three-state area. Lakes, streams and rivers, sand dunes, canals, forests, and wetlands abound. Quaint small towns, lighthouses, Amish communities, historical sites, and great bed and breakfasts round out the variety of attractions that make the Midwest a great destination in itself.

The region experiences four distinct seasons, although the further south one goes the more mild the winter weather. The weather dictates the cycling season, but the window of opportunity varies throughout the three states. Spring and fall require a jacket or extra layers in the more northerly regions, but nature's display of newly blooming flowers or brightly colored leaves makes the extra preparation worthwhile. Summer offers perhaps the best cycling weather, though humidity can be expected to raise the heat index. The warmer seasons linger longer and have an earlier onset in the southernmost areas of Ohio and Indiana. Hardier individuals may enjoy some of the cooler—but not overly cold—cycling days in the winters here.

While the cycling and scenery rank high, the most enticing attribute of the Midwest is its inhabitants. Known for their friendliness and eagerness to help, they will be glad to help you and advise you on what to do and see in their hometowns. The innkeepers exemplify this trait; take advantage of their hospitality.

Indiana

"'Hoosier' is not known with certainty. But certain it is that . . . Hoosiers bear their nickname proudly." — Meredith Nicholson

Indiana holds many surprises—architecturally rich towns, historic villages, and spectacular scenery. Amish communities, covered bridges, round barns, and lakes dot the landscape. You'll quickly realize that the state is not just cornfields; it offers a varied terrain that accommodates cyclists of all levels. Known as the "Crossroads of America," Indiana byways lead visitors to a multitude of attractions.

Wildlife and outdoors enthusiasts will enjoy the buffalo ranch and the many inland lakes in the northeastern corner of the state near Fremont. Boasting the nearby Indiana Dunes National Lakeshore, Aberdeen offers access to marked cycling routes as well as great mountain biking. Cole Porter aficionados and circus fans will want to make a beeline for charming Peru. Ligonier, once a large Jewish settlement, retains the impressive homes of the wealthy merchants who once settled here, a nice contrast to the more simple homes of the Amish who now inhabit the countryside. Another Amish stronghold, Berne has a Swiss flair and boasts a covered bridge and a round barn within biking distance of its city limits.

Bordering Lake Maxinkuckee, miniscule Culver, home to the Culver Academy, glows in the shadow of nearby Plymouth. The county has smartly developed a variety of signed cycling routes for visitors to explore the countryside. Charming Crawfordsville distinguishes itself with many historic buildings including the Lew Wallace Museum and a number of gracious homes.

Further south, Nashville takes on a truly southern feel; quaint shops dot its streets and hilly terrain reminds one of the southern mountains—a direct contrast with neighboring (and flat) Columbus, noted for its outstanding collection of architecture.

Since it seems to have stood still with time, the entire town of Metamora is listed on the National Historic Register. Centerville capitalizes on its antique shops and the interesting archways that highlight historic buildings throughout the town.

A true study in contrasts, Indiana warmly welcomes visitors to examine its many attractions in an up-close and personal manner. What better way to see it all than from the seat of a bicycle?

Always Inn

8072 East State Road
Nashville, IN 47448
Phone: (812) 988-2233
Fax: (812) 988-9550
E-mail: innkeeper@alwaysinn.com
Web: www.alwaysinn.com
Innkeeper: Deborah Epperson
Rates: Budget to Moderate

"The next morning the whole world, and I, too, had undergone a transformation. As I walked outdoors, I found myself transported back into a period of long ago, quite remote from the one I had left barely twelve hours before. How out of the ordinary the little hamlet was! Such charm! Such quaintness!"
— Selma Neubacher Steele, April 10, 1907. From *The House of the Singing Winds: Life and Work of T.C. Steele*; Selma N. Steele, Theodore L. Steele, and Wilbur B. Peat

In the early 1900s, artists established a colony in the Nashville, Indiana, area because of the inspiration provided by nature. T.C. Steele, quoted above, was involved in the development of a local artists' retreat. Today, Nashville retains the quaintness that Selma Neubacher Steele was so taken with in 1907. Charming storefronts, a nearby covered bridge, and a landscape punctuated by hills and "hollers" presents a picture-perfect setting for a challenging cycling odyssey.

Located halfway between Columbus and Nashville, The Always Inn shrouds itself in a lovely forest setting. Perched high upon a hill and nestled in the woods, this retreat lets you escape from the rigors of everyday life. The mood of this modern chalet is decidedly casual, with a "just like home" atmosphere.

The inn spans three levels and offers seven guestrooms, most of which contain a sofa bed to accommodate additional guests and are furnished with antiques from the Dodge Mansion in Detroit. Deborah Epperson, recently taking the reins as innkeeper, is constantly adding her own touches to personalize this wooded re-treat. She can provide a plethora of amenities—including a cham-pagne breakfast, anniversary or birthday dinners, or picnic bas-kets filled with local specialties—limited only by your imagination.

The enormous White Pine Room occupies the bottom level of the inn and provides plenty of space for stretching out. At one end is a king-size brass bed, while a living area with a brown marble fireplace occupies the other. The sofa and chaise provide extra sleeping space for a group of friends or family. A tiny bathroom with shower is tucked away into a niche in the room. Floral ac-cessories accent the décor in the winter-white rooms throughout the entire inn.

Also on the ground floor, The Trillium Room is decorated in a light sand color with brown carpet. An antique wooden double bed is covered with a white ring quilt; a sofa bed provides seating and additional sleeping. The good-sized room is also furnished with an antique record player and sewing machine. To complete the look with a unique and clever decorating trick, the shower curtain is made from a quilt.

On the second level, the modest sized Silver Birch room looks out over the woods. Its pine queen-size bed is covered with several pillows in teal, brown, and blue to coordinate with the bedspread. This room, with its antique dresser, conveys a more masculine sense than the other rooms. There is a bathroom with a shower.

A private balcony, black marble fireplace, and queen fourposter bed set the mood in the Monet Room, a large room decorated in pastel florals with impressionist art on the walls and an impres-sive view. A sofa bed and chair provide additional seating, and the bathroom has a shower and pedestal sink.

The Red Bud Suite on the upper level has two bedrooms that share a full bath. One bedroom has two pine queen beds with a sofa. The color scheme is neutral, with floral bed coverings. Just around the corner, the second bedroom has a full antique brass bed, a comfy chair, and a balcony that overlooks the woods and pond where you can enjoy a symphony of crickets, frogs, and birds. The suite is ideal for a family or group of friends.

Common features throughout the inn include private baths, candy dishes, TV and VCR in each room (with a large video library), central heating and air, and an outdoor hot tub to soothe your muscles after a ride. A nice selection of toiletries has been thoughtfully provided in all the bathrooms. A pond and plenty of room to roam on the grounds complete the picture.

Breakfast is served in the second-level dining room, which is part of the great room. On warm days you can eat on the balcony, where there are several tables. The great room includes a fireplace, stereo TV, piano, and Victorian furniture. The wrap-around deck is a perfect place to relax.

Reading through the guest journal, we noticed that many guests were first-time visitors and enjoyed their stay at this inn so much that they would use this experience as the standard by which to judge other inns. As this is an extremely popular tourist region, it is absolutely necessary to book in advance during the high season, which lasts from late spring through leaf peeping season. There are helpful tourist offices both here and in Columbus that will gladly offer suggestions for the multitude of diversions in the area.

Cycling from Always Inn

Neither of the following rides originates from the Always Inn. One starts in Nashville and the other at the Bartholomew County Fairgrounds. Highway 46, the location of the inn, carries heavy traffic and cannot be recommended as a cycling route. Brown County State Park is very scenic, but we can't recommend cycling it during peak tourist season. The roads are hilly, winding, and narrow. It would be incredibly unpleasant having to stop behind bumper-to-bumper traffic on the steep downhill sections, one of which has a sign warning cyclists to dismount to descend. On the other hand, low season cycling through here would be challenging, and unimpeded by traffic jams.

Terrain: The ride to Bean Blossom from Nashville is hilly with winding roads throughout—a really fun but challenging ride. The Columbus ride is much more gentle with some rolling hills.

Road Conditions: Mostly paved, but there is short steep stretch of gravel after the Bean Blossom Bridge.

Traffic: Light.

Mountain Biking Opportunities: Gnaw Bone Camp offers 25 miles of trails geared to various skill levels and is open to the general public; the fee is about $3.00. From the Always Inn, head toward Nashville and turn left on SR 135. Go about 2.5 miles and the camp is on the left. Phone (812) 988-4852 for more information.

Local Bike Shop
Bicycle Station
1005 25th Street
Columbus, IN 47201
(812) 379-9005

Nashville Hills Loop (23 miles)
Prepare for a very hilly ride on rural roads. The hills in the area provide scenic vistas; many log cabins concealed in the woods become obvious as you spin slowly by. The twisting route follows creeks and visits tiny hamlets. Pay special attention at the BR and BL spots—this area definitely does not follow the grid system.

To reach the start of this ride, turn left on US 46 from the Always Inn, continue to Route 135 North and turn right to go to downtown Nashville (*note:* Route 135 goes left to Gnaw Bone a few miles before reaching the right turn into Nashville. Don't turn left. Continue on US46 until coming to a T. Turn right here). There are several parking lots in Nashville.

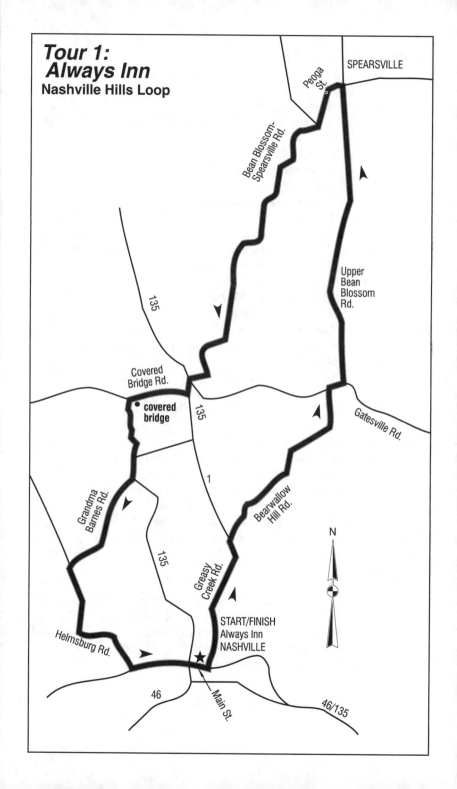

Tour 1:
Always Inn
Nashville Hills Loop

Cume	Turn	Street/Landmark
0.0		Start at the intersection of Van Buren and East Main in Nashville
0.2	L	**Greasy Creek**
2.2	R	**Bearwallow Hill**
5.2	R	**Gatesville**
5.6	L	**Upper Bean Blossom**
10.3	L	**Peoga** (Spearsville)
12.4	BL	**Spearsville** (this changes to **Bean Blossom**)
13.0	BR	Stay on **Bean Blossom**
13.2	BR	Stay on **Bean Blossom**
14.6	BR	Stay on **Bean Blossom**
14.7	BL	Stay on **Bean Blossom**
16.0	L	**Rt. 135** (*Caution*)
16.5	R	**Covered Bridge**—this is the Bean Blossom Bridge
17.1	L	No name road—short stretch of gravel here
17.6	R	**Rt. 135**
17.9	R	**Grandma Barnes**
20.6	L	**Helmsburg**
22.7	S	**Main St.** Downtown Nashville

Columbus Loop (23 miles)

Heading east to Columbus along route 46, you'll notice that the terrain here contrasts immensely with the rugged land in Nashville. Columbus is renowned for its fine collection of outstanding architecture and exemplifies what a forward-thinking community can do to maintain and improve its quality of life. Don't miss the guided architectural tour offered by the tourist office, which features buildings designed by the Saarinens, I.M. Pei, Weese and others.

For ice cream lovers, be sure to seek out Zaharako's on Washington Street in Columbus, where they make their own hot fudge. An attractive soda fountain salvaged from the World's Fair and made from Mexican onyx marble dominates the interior. After biking the area, you deserve this special treat.

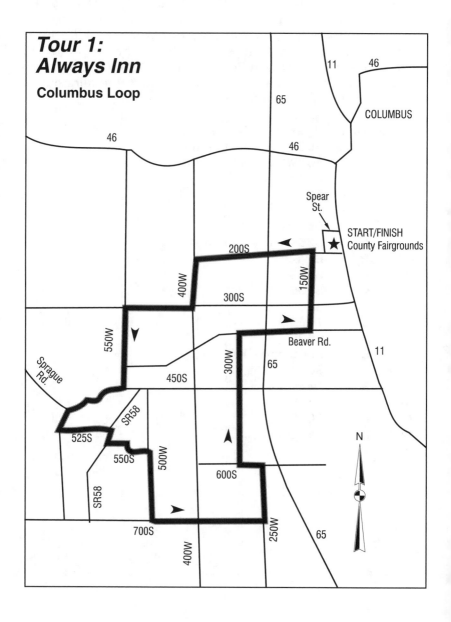

Tour 1:
Always Inn

Columbus Loop

This route was developed by the Columbus Cycling Club. The area is quite rural and the terrain is very gentle. There is parking at the County Fairgrounds, the starting point for this trip. To reach the fairgrounds, turn left out of the Always Inn on US 46. Follow this until you reach Route 11. Turn right. Go a short way and turn right on Spear. This winds through the fairgrounds. There are places close to Route 200S for parking.

Cume	Turn	Street/Landmark
0.0	R	**200S** from the fairground
2.7	L	**400W** curves left
3.7	R	**300S**
5.2	L	**550W**
6.7	R	**450S**
8.2	L	**Sprague**
8.6	L	**525S** (no sign here)
9.8	R	**SR 58**
10.1	L	**550S**
10.6	L	**550S**
11.1	R	**500W**
12.5	L	**700S**
15.1	L	**250W**
16.1	L	**600S** curve left
16.6	R	**300W**
19.2	R	**Deaver**
20.6	L	**150W**
22.3	R	**200S**
22.4	L	Fairground

Cole House

27 East Third Street
Peru, IN 46970
Ph: (765) 473-7636
Fax : (765) 472-2273
Innkeepers: Miles and Peggy Straly
Rates: Budget

Oh, the moonlight's fair tonight along the Wabash,
From the fields there comes the breath of new-mown hay,
Through the sycamores the candlelights are gleaming,
On the banks of the Wabash, far away.
Many years have passed since I strolled by the river,
Arm in arm, with sweetheart Mary by my side,
It was there I tried to tell her that I loved her,
It was there I begged of her to be my bride.
Long years have passed since I strolled thro' the churchyard.
She's sleeping there, my angel, Mary dear,
I loved her, but she thought I didn't mean it,
Still I'd give my future were she only here.

— Official State Song of Indiana

Situated on the Wabash River, the small town of Peru lays claim to a diverse assortment of historic figures and attractions. The most widely recognized native son is probably the composer and lyricist, Cole Porter, who spent his childhood here. His grandfather, J.O. Cole, built the Second Empire-style mansion on East Third Street now known as the Cole House. Situated right in town, the Cole House secures a dominant position in the commercial area of town. Convenient to restaurants and shops, it is within perfect walking distance of the downtown area.

The wealthiest man in Peru, J.O. Cole spared no expense in the process of building his home: exotic hardwoods, majestic fireplaces, high, ornamentally plastered ceilings with chandeliers, and a magnificent staircase demonstrate a rich sense of style. You'll immediately notice the patterned parquet floor when you step into the entryway; each room has its own distinctive pattern of inlaid wood. Because the downstairs is sparsely furnished, the enormity of these rooms makes a striking impression.

The guest quarters are all located on the second floor, each occupying one of the four corners of the house. We stayed in the Rose of Indiana, a pleasant and large room with a cozy alcove that adds architectural interest to the floral-themed décor; beige, black, pink, and green are the dominant colors. The antique walnut double bed is complemented with other antique furnishings and covered with a quilt and black throw pillows. The room's furnishings are reminiscent of an antique needlepoint cushion or handbag—practical and old-fashioned. The private bath, long and narrow with a clawfoot tub, tempts the weary cyclist to soak away any aches and pains. The white lace-covered shower curtain hints at an air of luxurious relaxation.

Kate's Cove, just down the hall, has a subtle mix of beige, pink, and lilac tones which paint a very feminine picture. The atmosphere is further enhanced by the bed quilt and bed skirt, which add even more feminine touches. A queen-size antique sleigh bed, table and chairs, and mirrored dresser round out the room. The lilac color scheme, which flaunts deep lilac walls with white, pink, and green accents throughout, is carried over into the private bath.

The Old Fashioned Garden is an appropriate name for a guestroom with a floral motif. Simple and pleasant, the room is furnished with two white wicker queen-size beds, green carpet, and white eyelet window coverings to suggest a garden setting. White eyelet bed skirts complement the window coverings and add a touch of airiness to the room, enhanced by the sea green, pink, and white hues. The private bath contains original fixtures, including an unusual bottom-filling clawfoot tub.

The J.O. Cole Suite duplicates the decorating scheme a man of means—like its namesake—might prefer. Definitely masculine in character, dark and regal hues color the opulent room, which is furnished with antique velvet chairs and built-in cedar closets. A sitting room provides an area to read, relax, or watch television. The private bath is done in tones of taupe and white and the shower has a Battenburg lace curtain.

Breakfast is served downstairs in a grand dining room. Like most of the house, this room has incredible woodworking throughout, as well as a buffet, china cabinet, Chinese screen, and large table. A fascinating Venetian chandelier serves as the light source. Breakfast is served on fine china, exactly what you would expect in such grand surroundings.

The large common area also serves as a second dining room (The innkeepers also host functions such as weddings, showers, and special events). This room also has its own unique parquet floor, heavy moldings, a fireplace with a mirror above the mantle, and two chandeliers.

If, after your stay at The Cole House, you're interested in learning more about the early life of Cole Porter, the local visitor's bureau has put together a driving tour that highlights significant sites related to the composer. Just be aware that most of the buildings on the tour are private, and trespassing is forbidden.

Another unusual local attraction in Peru is the Circus Hall of Fame. For ten weeks throughout the summer you can attend circus performances. In mid-July, the Circus City Festival—the second largest festival in the state—offers amateur circus performances. For those interested in airplanes and Air Force history, the Grissom Air Force Museum is the place to go.

Biking from The Cole House

The area surrounding Peru varies from relatively flat to moderately rolling. In the direction of the reservoir, you will find interesting rock formations that Native Americans used as a landmark on their water routes. The reservoir itself offers plenty of water recreation as well as spots for picnicking.

Going toward Wabash, the terrain becomes very rolling. Wabash, the county seat, has interesting architecture and a genuine small-town feel. Concerts and lectures take place at the Honeywell Center.

If these routes don't provide enough exercise for you, sit down and chat with innkeeper Miles Straly. He has helped organize a local cycling event and can suggest further riding possibilities in the area.

Terrain: Varies from flat to hilly.

Road Conditions: Good.

Traffic: A bit congested in towns and very light elsewhere.

Nearest Bike Shop
Breakway Bike Shop
154 North Grant Street
Peru, IN 46970-1903
Phone: (765) 473-3848

Historic Route to Mississinewa Lake (22.1 miles)
Along this route you will visit several sites important in the history of Miami County. Just before crossing the bridge out of town, you'll notice the tollhouse for the Wabash and Erie Canal. Built in 1840, it is the oldest structure of historic importance in Peru.

Next, you'll see a large rock that designates the location of the Osage Indian village. A plaque describes a bit of the history of the area and tribe. The Seven Pillars is a unique geological formation that served as a landmark along the river; today it provides a good photo opportunity. Mississinewa Lake was formed by a reservoir built in the 1960s. You'll see directional signs pointing the way to the many units of the park in the area. The terrain on this route is flat to gently rolling.

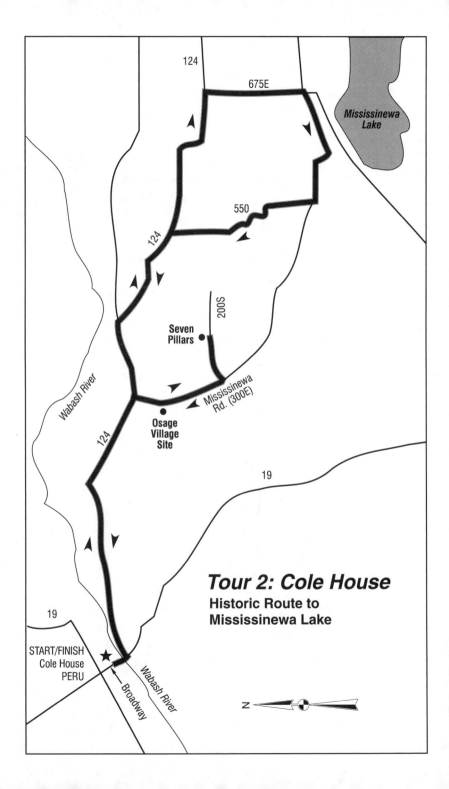

124

675E

Mississinewa Lake

124

550

200S

Seven
Pillars ●

Wabash River

Mississinewa Rd. (300E)

124

● Osage
Village
Site

19

Tour 2: Cole House
**Historic Route to
Mississinewa Lake**

19

START/FINISH
Cole House
PERU

Wabash River

Broadway

N

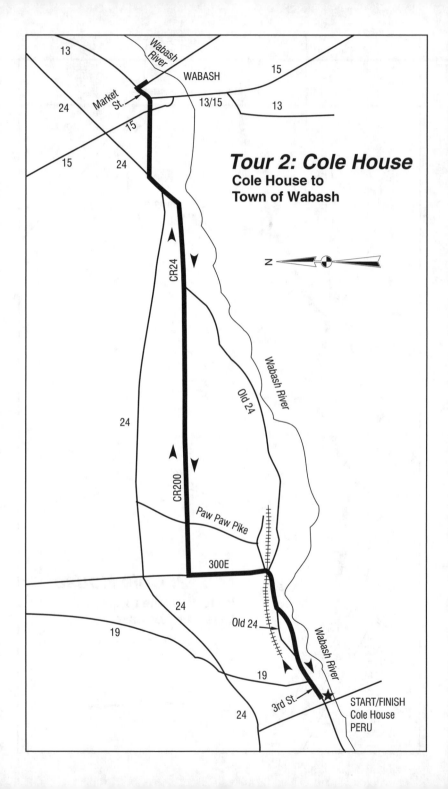

Cume	Turn	Street/Landmark
0.0	R	**Wabash**
0.1	R	**Canal**
0.2	L	**Broadway**
0.3	L	**SR 124**
2.8	R	**300E (Mississinewa Rd.)**
3.1	-	Site of **Osage Village**
4.1	L	**200S**
5.4	TA	and go back on **200S. Seven Pillars**
6.7	R	**300E**
7.9	R	**SR 124**
9.5	BR	at Y junction
12.3	R	**675E** (*note:* this is the start of a 2-hour hiking trail)
13.5	R	**Unmarked road**
14.9	R	**550**
18.7	L	**SR 124**
21.3	R	**Broadway**
21.4	L	**Canal**
21.9	R	**Wabash**
22.1	L	**Cole House**

Cole House to town of Wabash (29 miles)

What a shock that the terrain on this route contrasts immensely with the first route. Be prepared for some short and steep climbs. The town of Wabash warrants a visit. City parks provide spots for a picnic or restaurants are also available. This is an out-and-back ride.

0.0	R	**3rd**
0.9	L	**Canal**
1.0	R	**Paw Paw Pike** (cross Old 24 and railroad tracks)
3.2	L	**CR 300E**
4.5	R	**CR 200**
10.5	S	**CR 24** (Old 24)
12.1	R	**Mill**
13.8	BL	**Market**
14.4	R	**Wabash**
14.5	-	Courthouse at Wabash and Main

Cume	Turn	Street/Landmark
14.6	R	**Market**
15.2	BR	**Mill**
16.9	L	**CR 24**
18.5	S	**CR 200**; keep right at Y junction
24.5	L	**CR 300E**
25.8	S	**Paw Paw Pike** (Cross RR tracks and Old 24, continue on Paw Paw)
27.8	L	**Canal**
27.9	R	**3rd**
29.0		**Cole House**

Culver Bed & Breakfast

213 Lakeshore Drive
Culver, IN 46511
Phone: (219) 842-4009
Innkeepers: Carl and Chris Landskron
Rates: Budget to Moderate

> *"The room within is the great fact about the building."*
> — Frank Lloyd Wright

L ocated in the heart of Culver, Indiana, the Arts-and-Crafts-style Culver House Bed and Breakfast is being carefully redecorated by its new owners. Chris Landskron, the hostess, operates her own interior design business, so she knows what she is doing. Her creative flair is evident throughout this warm and cheerful home.

When you walk into the front entryway, you'll immediately notice that the tiny area sports a whimsical golf theme. Throughout the first floor, the natural wood flooring has been maintained, as well as the rich tones of the woodworking and built-in cabinets with leaded glass. Chris likes antiques and you will find many throughout the inn. But don't worry about sitting on one of the chairs or sofas—this is not a decorator showplace where you can look, but not touch; everything is here for your enjoyment.

The large but cozy living room has a lovely fireplace to take away the chill on a cool morning or evening. You can mingle here with other guests or retreat to the enclosed porch, which is replete with windows and has its own fireplace. The dining room has a beamed ceiling and spectacular built-in cabinetry. The oak mission-style furniture completes the look of this very comfortable room.

Upstairs, four bedrooms are open to guests. The entire second floor is covered with a neutral carpet that complements the décor in all the rooms. When the Landskrons bought the Culver house, they acquired a five-bedroom inn. But since one room was so small that the previous owner had cut off the end of a bed to make it fit in the minuscule room, the new owners decided to convert it into a lounge. Decorated to resemble hot air balloons, with a ceiling wallpapered with a blue sky and cloud pattern, the room inspires guests to dream about adventure. Or at least it distracts you while you sip your coffee, have a beverage, or select something from the book shelf or magazine rack. The lounge is equipped with a refrigerator, coffee maker, and water cooler.

Two of the rooms share an adjoining bath that was in the process of being remodeled during our stay. Having seen some of the results of Chris's decorating abilities, this will surely be a pleasant space. Grandma's Room, facing the street, has a medallion surrounding the ceiling fixture and contains a full-size antique walnut bed and other antique furnishings.

Jenny's Room, at the back of the house, lacked a focal point, so Chris needed something to liven up the room. She accomplished this by making the ceiling the prominent feature. She has patterned together several different wallpapers to create an interesting design that grabs the attention of guests. From your brass double bed, you can observe the intricate details of this special effect.

Across the way, there are two large suites. The North Room has a queen bed and is full of windows, which Chris has covered with pleated shades. The rattan furniture in the seating area offers a comfortable place for reading or relaxing. The sofa hides a queen-size bed. A small café table is perfect for morning tea or coffee; a coffee maker is provided in the room. Wallpaper with large stripes in several tones graces the walls, while attractive antique lamps accentuate the décor. Behind the bed, a portion of the wall is painted green and blue to serve as a headboard. A ceiling fan supplements the air conditioning for those days when a cross breeze from the windows makes for a refreshing and comfortable sleep.

The Lake Room, next door, has a queen-size canopy bed and white wicker furniture topped with floral-print cushions. The sofa converts to a queen-size sleeper to accommodate additional guests.

Paul Brent seashore designs reinforce the theme of being beside the water; to see the real thing you can visit the lakeside park just a short stroll away. The private bath has a shower dispenser that provides toiletries.

Chris will serve a tasty breakfast in the dining room whenever it is convenient for you. Over breakfast, she will be glad to relate the story of her first day in the B&B and her special guest—a food writer. The local dining scene also includes the Edgewater Café, located right in town. The menu is extensive and includes a 24-oz. steak for those who have worked up an appetite on the bike. Another spot in town that was recommended by Larry, the owner and cook at the Edgewater, is the Corn Dance, in downtown Culver.

The house has some history of its own: It seems that one of the previous residents, after moving out of state, earned a reputation as a black widow. A book was written on the topic, with photos of the Culver House years ago.

Biking from Culver Bed and Breakfast
The first bike route passes through the countryside of Marshall County, which is well known for its blueberry festival. On this route you will find Ancilla College, a round barn, and you'll be close to the Menominee statue, a tribute to an Indian chief.

The second route takes you on a short ride around the lake with plenty of places to stop and enjoy the scenery. Culver Academy is a private military school that is home to the Black Horse Cavalry, the largest such group in the U.S. The campus features outstanding architecture and offers guided tours of the campus, which is the second-largest of any educational institution in Indiana. After leaving the campus area, you will skirt the lake for awhile, with spectacular old cottages always in sight. The route briefly deviates from the lakeside, but eventually returns.

Plymouth, which is not on either route but can be reached by following the marked county routes, is a picturesque village with many splendid houses. The visitor's bureau will gladly make suggestions for diversions in the area.

Terrain: Flat to gently rolling.

Road Conditions: Good.

Traffic: Light.

Nearest Bike Shop
Country Road Bicycles & Fitness
201 East Garro
Plymouth, IN 46563
Phone: (219) 936-3334

Culver B&B to Ancilla (35.3 miles)
It's a simple matter to get into the country from Culver. This tour follows part of a marked route; if you want to go a longer distance, simply continue to follow the signs, which all form a loop. Along the way you will see the Menominee monument in the distance, and you'll pass close by Ancilla College—be sure to stop and see the chapel—and a round barn. (*Note:* In the following cue sheet, "B" roads run parallel to whichever road it notes, i.e., West 9th B runs parallel to West 9th Street between West 9th and West 10th).

Cume	Turn	Street/Landmark
0.0	L	Lakeshore
0.1	R	School
0.9	L	W. 17th
1.4	R	S. Thorn
3.4	R	15th
3.8	L	S. Tulip
4.3	L	W. 14th B
6.3	R	Marshall County Line Rd.
8.9	R	W. 12th
9.6	L	S. Upas
11.3	L	W. 10th B
12.2	R	Marshall County Line Rd.
13.2	R	W. 9th B
14.9	R	W. 9th

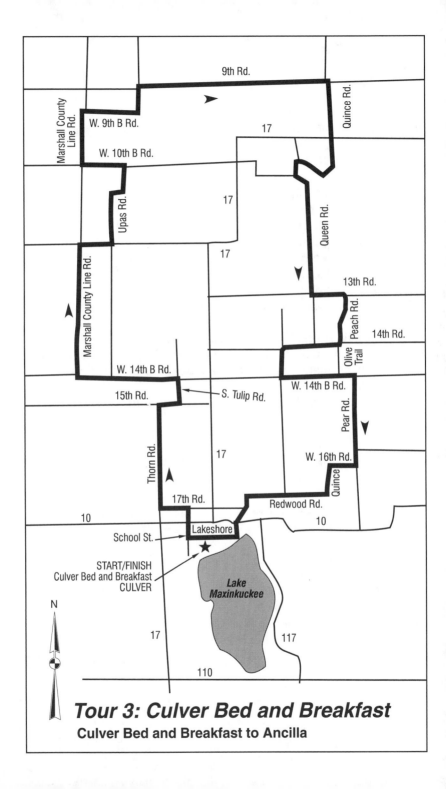

Tour 3: Culver Bed and Breakfast

Culver Bed and Breakfast to Ancilla

Cume	Turn	Street/Landmark
18.9	R	N. Quince
21.2	L	Queen
24.2	L	W. 13th
25.0	R	Peach
25.9	L	W. 14th
27.1	R	Olive Trail
27.7	R	14th B
28.8	L	Pear
30.6	R	W. 16th
31.2	BL	Quince
32.7	L	Redwood
34.0	R	Rt. 10
34.5	L	Lakeshore
35.3	L	Culver Bed & Breakfast

Around Lake Maxinkuckee (10.3 miles)

This ride is short but sweet—and scenic. Stop and spend some time at Culver Academy, which welcomes guests and gives guided tours of the grounds. Stately mansions line the lake. If only we could all live and ride in such pleasant surroundings!

Cume	Turn	Street/Landmark
0.0	R	Lakeshore
0.8	R	Rt. 10
1.7	R	Rt. 117
5.7	R	20th B
6.2	R	S. Shore
7.3	R	S. Sycamore
8.0	R	S. Sage
9.2	R	South
9.4	L	Wabash
9.5	R	Obispo
9.7	L	**Davis**, then a quick
	R	onto **S. Main**
10.2	R	Lakeshore
10.3	R	Culver Bed & Breakfast

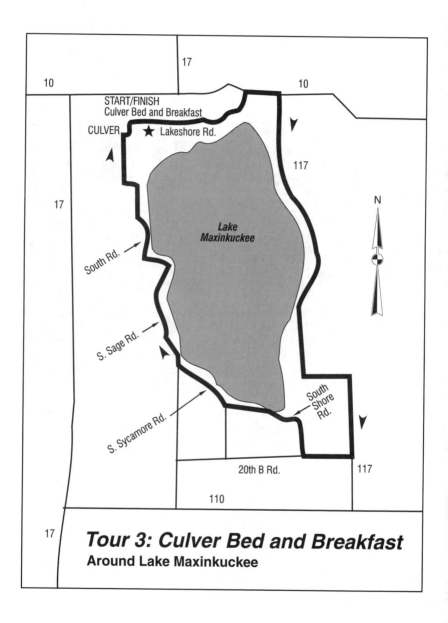

17

10

10

START/FINISH
Culver Bed and Breakfast

CULVER ★ Lakeshore Rd.

117

17

South Rd.

Lake
Maxinkuckee

N

S. Sage Rd.

S. Sycamore Rd.

South
Shore
Rd.

117

20th B Rd.

110

17

Tour 3: Culver Bed and Breakfast
Around Lake Maxinkuckee

The Historic Lantz House, in Centerville, Indiana, is notable for the archway in the center of its façade, a rarity in this part of the country.

Historic Lantz House

214 Old National Road
Centerville, IN 47330
Phone: (765) 855-2936; (800) 495-2689
Innkeeper: Marcia Hoyt
Rates: Budget

"In my old town, as in many others, it became 'Main Street' for a few blocks, but both east and west it quickly resumed the nominal dignity of its national character." — William Basard Hale in *The Century Magazine,* Dec. 1911, No. 2

Tucked into a few blocks along the historic National Road, the quaint town of Centerville has been welcoming travelers since pioneers passed through on their way to settle the West. The once-bustling town still maintains a sense of its former self. Federal, Greek Revival, and Italianate architecture dominates the streetscape, but if you look closely you will find the old Salisbury Court House (a log cabin) located behind the Mansion House. You can see several of these architectural styles and learn a bit about old Centerville and the National Road if you follow the town's walking tour. Just up the road in Richmond, you'll spot one of the twelve Madonna of The Trail monuments, erected as a tribute to the pioneer women who traversed this new road to the West.

Today, visitors come to Centerville because of its many antique malls—it claims the largest in the state, country, or world depending on which brochure you read. The excellent and extremely helpful visitor center in Richmond can help you with local points of interest.

Whether you've come for the history or the antique malls, you'll find appropriate accommodations at the Historic Lantz House. This building was an important stop for travelers on the National Road, as Mr. Lantz operated a wagon building business from here. Described in the brochure as "a simply elegant bed & breakfast," this brick federal-style inn is notable for the archway that acts as a focal point on the façade. A rare architectural feature in this part of the country, the arch on the Historic Lantz House is one of five in Centerville.

The cordial hostess, Marcia Hoyt, returned to her roots in Centerville after a long absence. She restored the house in a style appropriate to the period; the results depict another era, transporting the guest back into time. If you can find a copy of the December, 1996, issue of *Midwest Living*, you'll get a glimpse of both the welcoming Marcia and the appealing living room.

As you enter the foyer, the first thing that catches your eye is the black and white painted floor. To the left, the large living room has high ceilings and is furnished with a sofa and chairs, presenting itself as the perfect place to browse through one of the many books available for your reading pleasure. And if it is cool enough, you can read in front of the fire without the distraction of a TV. Background music comes from a central sound system. The dining room, adjacent to the living room, contains a table that comfortably seats six. Here Marcia serves a delectable breakfast which reveals her culinary expertise. A china cabinet graces one of the walls of this room, displaying Marcia's collection of bowls.

The staircase from the foyer leads to the four guestrooms and another common area with a large collection of books and a TV. Marcia sets out hot beverages here, so you can watch the morning news and sip your coffee or tea. All rooms have central air, smoke detectors, and secure locks.

At the top of the stairs, separate from the other guestrooms, is the grand Hamiltonian room, with windows facing front and back. The Queen canopy bed, covered with a quilt, is the focal point of this spacious room. The brown wide-plank floor is covered with a deep green area rug. There is a desk for writing or spreading out your maps, as well as comfortable chairs to sit in and read. An especially interesting touch, the twig chair on the non-working fireplace mantel is draped with mini-lights that give the room a special glow.

The other guestrooms are located in a separate part of the house. Passing through another common area with a TV, games, and books, you'll reach Melissa's room. Facing the street, the room is furnished with a pair of twin beds (which can be made into a king), two chairs, and a desk. White quilts on green beds give the room a clean, crisp look.

The Cardinal room—like the others in this wing—is covered with berber carpet. Dominating the room is a queen-size bed with a wooden headboard and white bedspread, along with a sofa where you can stretch out and read a book from the nearby bookcase. A sink and vanity complete the room, and of course, there is a private bath.

The Edenwood room, with its brass double bed and antique writing desk, is agreeably decorated in subtle tones. This room would be the perfect place to spend time writing a novel.

Behind the inn, a wonderful garden complements the atmosphere of the house, enticing guests to relax and enjoy the surroundings. You'll feel equally at ease here as you do within the confines of the inn.

Marcia is committed to her community and involved in several projects. She contributed to the town walking tour and is a fount of information about the National Road, which has been designated a National Scenic Byway. If you can catch her when she is not busy readying the inn, she will update you on the projects in which she takes a special interest.

If you're looking for dining recommendations, Marcia will direct you to a variety of restaurants to suit any budget. The Olde Richmond Inn, one of her dinner favorites, is located in the historic area of nearby Richmond and certainly merits a visit. Remember that many Amish restaurants—and other businesses as well—are closed on Sundays.

Biking from the Historic Lantz House

For the cyclist, quiet roads lead to the Amish country, orchards, and historic communities. Abington, surrounded by hills on all sides, boasts several historic buildings. A short detour will lead to a round barn. North of Centerville, farm lanes pass through field after field in this decidedly agricultural region.

Terrain: The area varies greatly. Heading to Economy you'll encounter mostly flat terrain interspersed with some hills, especially a steep hill into Economy. On the Abington route, the hills begin on Pottershop Road with a very nice descent into Abington. Because of this, getting out of Abington means climbing. An out and back from the Lantz House would be a short and pleasant option.

Road Conditions: The roads are in good condition; all are paved.

Traffic: Roads are lightly traveled.

Mountain Biking Opportunities: Ask the staff of Ike's Bikes for recommendations.

Nearest Bike Shop

Ike's Motorcycle Sales, Inc. (They sell non-motorized bikes, too!)
111 South 6th Street
Richmond, IN 47374
Phone: (765) 962-3683

Centerville-Abington Route (24.9 miles)

This route passes by farms and does have some hills, especially in the southern portion. It seems that all roads lead out of (and up from) Abington, a sleepy town with a small general store that sells food and beverages. If you have the time, take the detour to see the round barn on County Road.

Cume	Turn	Street/Landmark
0.0	**R/L**	Right out of Lantz House and make a quick left on **Ash**
0.2	**R**	On **Blue and White**

Tour 4: Historic Lantz House
Centerville-Abington Route

START/FINISH
Historic Lantz House
CENTERVILLE

N. Morton Rd.

US 40

US 40

Colvin Rd.

Willow Grove Rd.

McConaha Rd.

N

Pennville Rd.

Three Mile Rd.

Kirlin Rd.

Willow Grove Rd.

Centerville Rd.

Potter Shop Rd.

general
store

(optional detour)

round barn

Willow Grove Rd.

ABINGTON

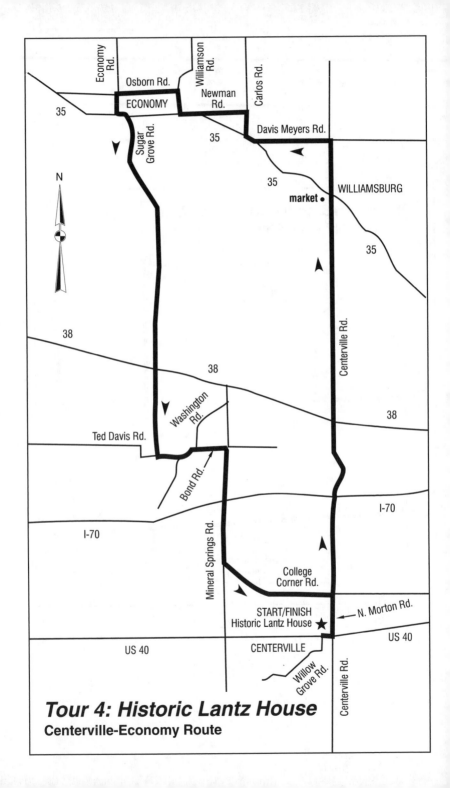

Economy Rd.

Osborn Rd.

Williamson Rd.

Carlos Rd.

Newman Rd.

ECONOMY

35

Davis Meyers Rd.

Sugar Grove Rd.

35

35

market ●

WILLIAMSBURG

N

35

38

Centerville Rd.

38

38

Washington Rd.

Ted Davis Rd.

Bond Rd.

I-70

I-70

Mineral Springs Rd.

College Corner Rd.

N. Morton Rd.

START/FINISH
Historic Lantz House ★

US 40

CENTERVILLE

US 40

Willow Grove Rd.

Centerville Rd.

Tour 4: Historic Lantz House
Centerville-Economy Route

Cume	Turn	Street/Landmark
0.3	L	**Willow Grove**
3.0	S	Changes to **Colbin**
4.4	R	**McConaha**
4.7	L	**Three Mile**
6.3	BR	To **Kirlin**
8.4	L	**Pennville**
10.7	L	**Pottershop Rd**.
14.5	-	*Detour to round barn:* Right on **Willow Grove**, go about a mile to **County Line**; you will see a round barn on your right. Go right for a better view of the barn, then re-trace your path back to this intersection)
18.4	L	**Abington**—general store on the right
18.6	BL	Sign says "Centerville"
24.8	L	**Main (US 40)**
24.9	R	Lantz House

Centerville-Economy (32.8 miles)

This route traverses farmland and Amish country, where you'll see an Amish woodworking shop and a natural produce shop along the way. Although basically flat, there are a few climbs. This ride is especially pleasant in the morning or early evening.

Cume	Turn	Street/Landmark
0.0	L	On **Main (US 40)** from the Lantz House
0.2	L	**N. Morton** (changes name to **Centerville**)
9.6	-	Town of Williamsburg; market on left
10.6	L	**Davis Meyers**
12.8	R	**US 35**; *caution*
12.9	R	**Carlos**
13.4	L	**Newman**
14.4	S	Onto **US 35**; *caution*
14.9	R	**Williamson**
15.4	L	**Osborn**
16.8	L	**Economy Rd.**; steep climb into Economy
17.3	L	**US 35**; caution
17.4	R	**Sugar Grove** (Sugar Grove Woodworks, Sugar Grove Natural Foods)

Cume	Turn	Street/Landmark
24.9	L	**Ted Davis**. *Caution* on Ted Davis Bridge; rough joints
25.5	L	**Washington**
26.0	S	Name changes to **Bond**
26.5	R	**Mineral Springs**
29.0	L	**College Corner**
29.2	BR	Stay on **College Corner**
31.7	R	**Centerville**
32.6	R	**Main (US 40)**
32.8	R	Lantz House

The Inn at Aberdeen
3158 South State Road 2
Valparaiso, IN 46383
Phone: (219) 465-3753
E-mail: innaberd@netnitco.net
Innkeepers: Linda and John Johnson
Rates: Moderate to Deluxe

We look to Scotland for all our ideas of civilisation.—Voltaire

Aberdeen, a new planned development in the northwest corner of Indiana, consists of shops, homes, and a golf course.
The highlight of the area is a tribute to the Scot's style of civiliza-
tion. A former farmstead that served as a hunting lodge, dairy
farm, and a horse farm, The Inn at Aberdeen experienced a meta-
morphosis from an already attractive farm house into a beautiful
inn. The original structure was enhanced with sympathetically-
designed additions that maintain the integrity of this historic
landmark.

When guests arrive at the door, they immediately receive a warm
and enthusiastic welcome from the staff. A bit different from a
traditional bed and breakfast, the Inn at Aberdeen nevertheless
affords an attentive and homey atmosphere, despite having eleven
guestrooms. While you are busy admiring the outstanding décor,
the curvaceous staircase, and the inviting atrium, the staff at
the desk will provide you with the details about your room.

The atrium, as its name suggests, embraces guests within its
light-filled confines, which are reminiscent of a gazebo. Here,
guests are invited to visit with others, help themselves to a beverage, or enjoy a snack. A decadent cheesecake that was available the night of our stay prompted a Pavlovian response and
offered an extra incentive to bike long and hard so that we could
indulge, guilt-free.

Also on the main floor, toward the rear of the inn, the bistro-style
kitchen serves scrumptious breakfasts to guests. The room is

bordered by shelves that hold a variety of teapots; one will be brought down to serve your tea if that is your preference. The green wrought iron tables complement the décor, as does the bar. We thoroughly enjoyed our breakfast of Aberdeen pancakes, a rich dish combining a traditional batter with sausage. We were shocked when other guests fretted about the richness of the dish— that style of food ranks high in the reasons to stay at a bed and breakfast establishment in the first place! The staff, without acting surprised or judgmental, went to the pantry to see what they had in stock and graciously made a breakfast to order for these calorie- and fat-counting guests. In addition to the delicious pancakes, tea and coffee, ice water, fresh-squeezed orange juice, and fresh fruit also graced the menu for the day. The kitchen is open to guests, and should you have a craving during the middle of the night, you will be served up something to please you.

A conference center is available for special occasions or business meetings—this would make an excellent place for a club meeting or special event.

The eleven guest suites come in several styles, most being a variation on a Queen Ann theme. This being the planned village of Aberdeen, all rooms bear a name that brings Scotland to mind.

The Alloway Suite contains a fully-equipped kitchen, making it a perfect spot for an extended stay. Equipped with everything you need to make yourself at home, this apartment-style suite also has its own private outside entrance. The bedroom contains a fourposter king-size bed and a whirlpool tub.

The Bannockburn Suite pays tribute to the Battle of Bannockburn, in which Robert the Bruce defeated Edward I in 1314, regaining the northern lands of Scotland. The suite, a very large and elegant area, has dark gray and green brocade-style wallpaper with a floral border. At one end of the room, an attractive fireplace is the focal point for a conversation area outfitted with two upholstered side chairs. Along another wall, an elegant desk serves as a spot for poring over cycling route maps or doing other work. Dominating the room is a grand fourposter king-size bed, accessed by wooden steps. Just through the door, a deck looks over the front gardens. The private bath appears to be as large as an ordinary bedroom. Outfitted with a two-person Jacuzzi, a free-standing shower, personal bath accessories, and two fluffy robes, this tiled retreat could be the only room you use throughout your stay. Other suites in the inn are patterned after this one and have similar layouts.

In the original part of the house, the Dunnotar Suite evokes Scotland with tartan plaids, wooden floors covered with runners, and a sports-themed border on the walls. A one-of-a-kind room, this retreat offers a private bath and can be combined with the Aberdeen Suite next door for a group or family.

The Aberdeen Suite boasts its own private entrance and contains a substantial living area furnished with dark rattan furniture and wing chairs. The wood flooring is set off by the stone fireplace, French doors, and green crown molding, which gives the room the air of a lovely country place in a verdant setting.

One of three suites that are similar in nature and contain two queen-size beds, The Edinburgh Suite has an off-white carpet throughout the room, wrought iron beds with romantic canopies, a fireplace sitting area, and a large spa-style bath complete with herbal bath treats and fluffy robes.

If you can tear yourself away from your luxurious surroundings, you'll find that the surrounding area has much to offer the visitor. The town of Valparaiso itself (referred to as "Valpo" by the locals) typifies a small and historic Indiana settlement. Antique and artisan shops—and of course, an ice cream parlor—line the downtown streets.

For nature lovers, the Indiana Dunes National Seashore is located just a short bike ride away. Picnicking, hiking, and even biking along the Calumet Trail are possible in this National Park Service unit. A comprehensive visitor's center explains the geology of the park. Beaches for swimming and picnicking dot the lakeshore. Of course, everybody needs to participate in one of the two dune climbs. Certain areas offer excellent birdwatching opportunities; the park covers over 14,000 acres of various ecosystems and certainly has enough diversions to keep one occupied for several days.

For those seeking other types of excitement, the South Shore Railroad goes to Chicago and Southbend. Casinos are scattered about the area for those wanting to try their luck at gambling.

Biking from The Inn At Aberdeen

Terrain: Basically flat.

Road Conditions: Very good.

Traffic: Mostly light, with an increase near towns.

Mountain Biking Opportunities: The Calumet Trail is unpaved. Prairie Duneland Trail extends 5.8 miles, and the Imagination Glen Park is a private area for off-road biking. Contact the Convention & Visitors Bureau for details.

Nearest Bike Shop
Buck's Bicycle Shop
610 Silhavy Road
Valparaiso, IN 46383
Phone: (800) 863-6593

The Inn at Aberdeen to Chesterton (31.4 miles)
This pleasant route travels along back roads to the delightful little town of Chesterton. From this point it is possible to continue on to the Dunes. The city park in town makes an excellent picnic spot.

Cume	Turn	Street/Landmark
0.0	R	**Aberdeen Dr.**
0.2	R	**Tower Rd.**, becomes **250W**
5.3	R	**550N**
7.2	L	**Goodric Rd.** curves into **75W** and **850N**

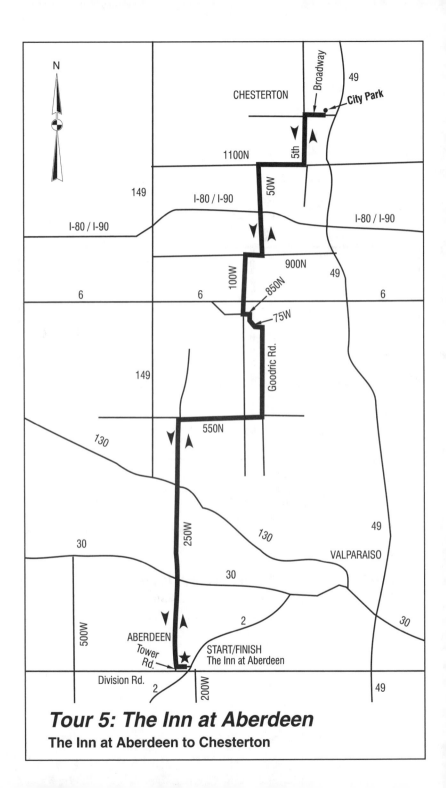

Tour 5: The Inn at Aberdeen
The Inn at Aberdeen to Chesterton

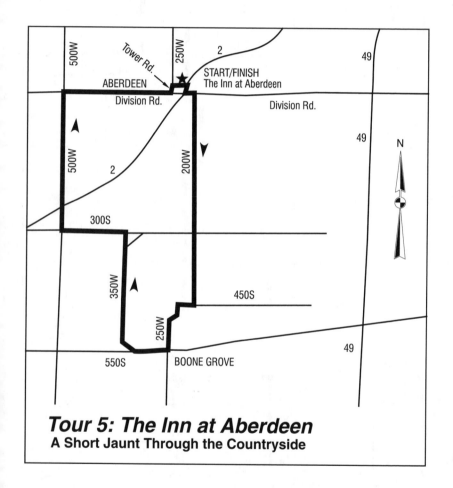

Tour 5: The Inn at Aberdeen
A Short Jaunt Through the Countryside

Cume	Turn	Street/Landmark
10.5	R	**100W**
11.0	R	**900N**
11.5	L	**50W**
13.4	R	**1100N**
14.4	L	**5th**
15.6	R	**Broadway**
15.7	-	City Park
15.8	L	**5th**
17.0	R	**1100N**
18.0	L	**50W**
19.9	R	**900N**
20.4	L	**100W**
20.9	L	**850N**
21.1	BR	**75W**
24.2	R	**550N**
26.1	L	**250W**, becomes **Tower Rd.**
31.2	L	**Aberdeen Dr.**
31.4		Inn at Aberdeen

A Short Jaunt Through the Countryside (17.0 miles)

The Inn at Aberdeen is located in the country, so an obvious route includes a pleasant tour of the countryside. The route is relatively flat with little traffic.

Cume	Turn	Street/Landmark
0.0	R	**SR 2**
0.4	L	**Division**
0.6	R	**200W**
5.0	R	**450S**, becomes **250W**
6.3	R	**550S**
7.2	R	**350W**, town of Boone Grove
9.3	S	at Y junction
9.6	L	**300S**
11.3	R	**500W**
14.0	R	**Division**
16.3	L	**Tower Rd.**
16.8	R	**Aberdeen Dr.**
17.0		The Inn at Aberdeen

The Metamora Inn, Metamora, Indiana

The Metamora Inn

P.O. Box 131
Wynn Street
Metamora, IN 47030
Phone: (765) 647-2176
E-mail: metamorainn@cnz.com
Web: www.metamorainn.com
Innkeepers: Ray and Pat Gulley & Family
Rates: Budget to Moderate

> *If I wait for tomorrow*
> *To come my way*
> *What if in my "Patience"*
> *I miss today?*
> — from "Patience," by Pat Gulley, Innkeeper

Don't wait for tomorrow to come to Metamora! This old canal town experienced a rebirth when much of the town was zoned commercial and a variety of establishments opened for business. Because a significant number of the buildings here are on the national historic register, the original character of this once-bustling town on the Whitewater Canal endures—much to the delight of visitors.

Conveniently located in the heart of the town, the Metamora Inn, a restored 1850s home, offers guests a comfortable stay in a choice of rooms. All rooms except for the suite are located on the ground floor, making this an ideal place for those who prefer not to climb stairs. Outside entrances leading to each room ensure the privacy of guests—there really is no common gathering room for guests to mingle other than the breakfast room.

The innkeepers reside off the premises, but the entire family is involved in the operation of the inn. Ray and son William did the renovation, daughter Colleen provides breakfast, granddaughter Katelyn serves the evening snack, and Pat provides the good conversation and warm welcome. Their commitment to and enthusiasm for this novel town shows in their animated discussions about life in Metamora. Besides the Metamora Inn, the Gulleys own several shops scattered throughout the village, and they will be offering additional rooms in another building that will serve as a bed and breakfast. Their boundless energy is inspirational.

The Gulleys currently have two houses available for guests. The Shepherd's House can host up to eight guests in this totally self-catering hostelry, which is the perfect place for a group or family wanting their own private residence for their visit.

Back at the Metamora Inn, the Suite Retreat is decorated in a retro '50s style and offers two rooms, each with full Hollywood beds. Blonde furnishings typical of the era; movie star pictures, a white vinyl chair, and leopard accents reproduce the décor of the decade. The bathroom is finished in brown and gray with lighthouse pictures throughout. This large retreat has plenty of space for four and may seem palatial for two people.

The three downstairs rooms match the creativity of the Suite Retreat. Clara's Room, at the back of the house, has an old-fashioned feel. Two antique double beds, beige floral wallpaper with complementing border, and an angel motif bestow upon this room a Victorian air. A wicker blanket chest offers an original seating option. The private bathroom has a shower, a coat rack, a brick-patterned linoleum floor, and lace-patterned wall coverings.
White wicker furniture and accessories are spread throughout the Sunshine and Wicker Room. Yellow flowered wallpaper topped with a border forms a wainscoting in this pale yellow room. The bathroom has a pink sink and even more white wicker accents. The bright and cheerful room has two full beds and can accommodate four people.

William's room, named for the Gulley's son, faces the street. A large room, it is wallpapered with a pine and berry pattern, with red molding and green accents. The fireplace with electric logs adds an essential element to this outdoors-themed room. Two antique metal beds, one twin and one full, comfortably accommodate three guests. The shelves in the decorative closet are laden with objects found in nature. Chairs and a bench provide seating.

Flowers dominate in the Three Sisters' Room, named in honor of the daughters. The flowered wallpaper with a contrasting border, green trim, and green carpet complete the lush garden theme. An electric log fireplace and decorative closet highlight the décor. The bathroom has a green marble linoleum floor with white linens.

After an exhausting day of cycling, you'll appreciate the snack and fancy coffee provided in each guestroom. Granddaughter Katelyn enjoys being involved in the operation, and delivers a tray of goodies to guests in the evening.

Breakfast is served in a separate dining area and Pat, the resident poet, will recite some of her verse for you. The excellent rolls are made by her daughter and sold at their bakery. Breakfast time is flexible, as long as you let Pat know your schedule. In keeping with the time-warp feeling of Metamora, be aware that this little area of Indiana does not abide by Daylight Savings Time.

Bicycling from Metamora Inn
Metamora is just one of the interesting towns in the region. The area offers scenic bike routes into such quaint towns as Oldenburg, the "Town of Spires," and Brookville, the county seat. When you reach the Oldenburg area you might do a doubletake when you look at the street names—for a moment you'll wonder if you have cycled into Germany. Settled by German immigrants, these small towns still have a distinctly German flavor. The rolling terrain and the redbuds blooming in spring paint a splendid picture of the valley. After your cycling adventure, take a ride on the canal boat, a scenic excursion train ride, or a jaunt in a horse and buggy.

Terrain: Hilly.

Traffic: Very little, except on the state routes.

Road conditions: Good.

Local Bike Shop
Bike Center
11 West Church Street
Oxford, OH 45056
Phone: (513) 523-4880

Metamora Inn to Brookville Reservoir (29.9 miles)
Quiet roads through scenic landscapes lead to the Brookville Reservoir. The descent to the reservoir is countered with an equally steep ascent out of the valley. A detour at Garr Hill Road leads to an attractive picnic area along the water. As an alternative to riding the roads back to the town of Brookville, you can use the bike path that begins nearby. Exercise caution coming down the hill into Brookville, as traffic seems to increase on this short section.

Cume	Turn	Street/Landmark
0.0		**Wynn**
0.1	**L**	**SR 52**
0.3	**R**	**Duck Creek**
1.2	**BR**	**Duck Creek**
5.5	**L**	**McRidge**
6.5	**L**	**Crossover**
7.0	**S**	**Rt. 1**
7.9	**R**	**Cause**; pop machine on right
13.0	-	**Klein Rd.**; store
14.5	**R**	**Rt. 101**
17.3	-	**Garr Hill Rd.** A right turn here will take you to the reservoir, adding about 3 miles to the distance
21.4	**S**	Stop sign. **Rt. 1**
21.7	**R**	**SR 52**
29.8	**L**	**Wynn**
29.9		Metamora Inn

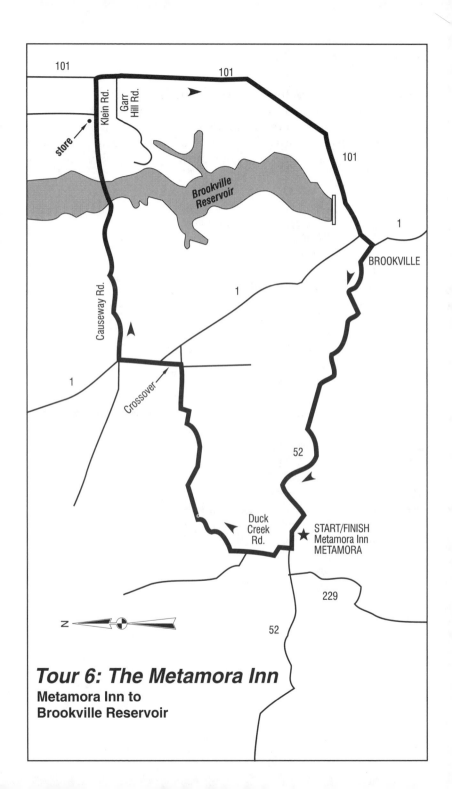

101

101

Klein Rd.

Garr Hill Rd.

101

store

Brookville Reservoir

1

BROOKVILLE

Causeway Rd.

1

Crossover

1

52

Duck Creek Rd.

START/FINISH
Metamora INN
METAMORA

229

N

52

Tour 6: The Metamora Inn

**Metamora Inn to
Brookville Reservoir**

Metamora Inn to Oldenburg (31.8 miles)

You will think that you are touring in Germany when you read the names of the streets in the area. The terrain is challenging, with some steep climbs. Check your odometer to keep track of where you are, as some signs are missing or so rusty that they are illegible.

Cume	Turn	Street/Landmark
0.0	R	**Wynn**
0.1	L	**SR 52**
0.9	L	**229.** Steep ascent
2.4	L	**Haytown Hill Rd.**
3.5	BL	**Haytown Hill Rd.**
4.6	R	**Pipe Creek Rd.**
5.3	BL	**Pipe Creek Rd.**
5.8	L	**Snail Creek** (illegible sign)
7.7	R	**Shop Rd.**
9.4	R	**St. Marys Rd.**
10.1	-	Oak Forest General Store
13.5	-	**St. Marys**: steep ascent, store, St. Mary's of the Rock Church
15.5	BR	**St. Marys**
15.7	BL	**St. Marys**
19.7	R	**Sawmill Rd.**
19.8	L	**VasserStrasse**
20.1	R	**Maulbeerfergenstrasse**
20.4	R	**Hauptstrasse (220)**; grocery store
26.0	-	Peppertown; steep descent
30.8	R	**SR 52**
31.7	R	**Wynn**
31.8		Metamora Inn

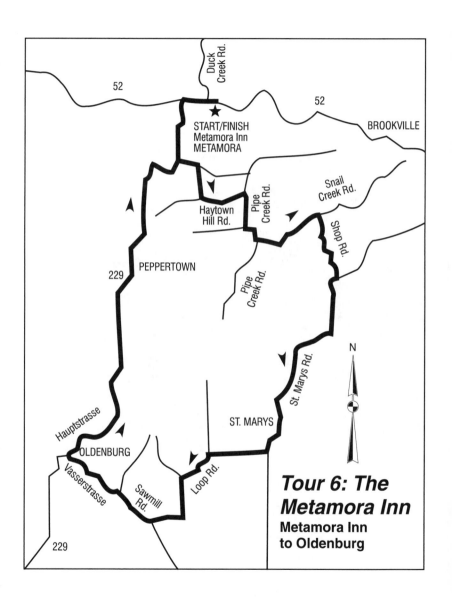

Duck Creek Rd.

52

52

BROOKVILLE

★

START/FINISH
Metamora Inn
METAMORA

Snail
Creek Rd.

Pipe Creek Rd.

Haytown
Hill Rd.

Shop Rd.

PEPPERTOWN

229

Pipe Creek Rd.

St. Marys Rd.

N

ST. MARYS

Hauptstrasse

OLDENBURG

Vasserstrasse

Sawmill
Rd.

Loop Rd.

Tour 6: The
Metamora Inn
**Metamora Inn
to Oldenburg**

229

Our Country Home, near Crawfordsville, Indiana

Our Country Home

c/o The Smith Family
P.O. Box 51762,
Indianapolis, IN 46251
Phone: (765) 794-3139
Fax: (765) 794-4997
Web: www.icatmall.com/ochome
E-mail: Ochome@lndy.tds.net
Innkeepers: Debbie and Randy Smith
Rates: Moderate

Have you heard of the wonderful one-hoss shay,
That was built in such a logical way,
It ran a hundred years to a day?
— Oliver Wendell Holmes

Innkeeper Deb Smith will tell you over the phone that Our Country Home is not an elegant place. This is a place to get away from the stress of the big city, to have some peace and quiet and to be part of the family. This is more in keeping with the British style of bed and breakfast; you will be sharing a room in a family home. The Smiths have plenty of space for guests, and they offer a level of hospitality that makes you feel as if you are good friends of the hosts. In fact, there is a plaque in the house that says: "Come as a guest, leave as a friend."

The Smiths have always lived in the country and can't understand the attraction of the city. Consequently, they want you to experience everything that country living has to offer. First is the peace and quiet: Though the small town of Crawfordsville is nearby, Our Country Home feels as though it is in the middle of nowhere, far from the hustle and bustle of the big city. There are plenty of diversions for guests. If you enjoy horses, you'll find a barnful out back. The Smiths will arrange a ride for you on a compatible horse. Trails on and near the property offer a quiet ride through the woods. If a carriage ride is more to your liking, the Smiths can arrange one; they own several carriages and specialize in providing transportation in these Amish-built buggies. Many people come just for the carriage rides, and many a couple has proposed along the way. If you prefer more physically demanding activities, you can help put up the hay. And if you *really* enjoy doing physically-demanding farm work, you can convince the Smiths to let you muck the stalls.

No matter what other activities you would like to participate in, you will find the hosts full of suggestions. But remember, you came here to bicycle and enjoy the bed and breakfast. The Smiths have thought about that too, and have bicycles for those guests who forgot to bring theirs.

The approach to the inn is via a long, hard-packed gravel driveway. If the hosts are at home, you will be greeted at the door; should your arrival time not coincide with their schedule, you are welcome to come in and make yourself at home until they return. From the start, they insist that you are a friend rather than a stranger.

The large two-story house contains several rooms for your relaxation. The first room that you will enter centers around a fireplace, with ample furnishings to stretch out and enjoy the warmth on a chilly evening. The adjacent room has books and more seating. A third room offers information on local activities and events and is the perfect place to plan your schedule for the next few days.

Meals are served in a large dining room that abuts a country kitchen with a center island. Guests can sit around the counter, drink coffee or tea, and chitchat with Deb while she prepares a hearty breakfast. The large dining table is necessary for the copious amounts of food that Deb prepares for this meal—one rule at Our Country Home is that no guest will be hungry. If the huge portions at breakfast haven't satisfied you, speak up and more will appear. On the other hand, if you are able to eat everything that is served, you have an insatiable appetite. When we saw the amount of food that Deb was preparing, we asked if perhaps a small army would be joining us for breakfast.

The first bedroom is decorated in a western style. Scattered throughout the room are animal skins, a cow skull that brings to mind a Georgia O'Keefe painting, Indian memorabilia, and cowboy hats. A Mickey Mouse ceiling fan and switch plate add a whimsical touch. Fluffy towels and toiletries are furnished, and Deb thoughtfully brought up a pitcher of ice water for evening refreshment.

The next room has a totally different feel, with nicely appointed furniture and a subtle touch of Victoriana, brightened by light-colored wallpaper. The third guestroom was occupied, so we got just a brief glance of the cannonball bed and bright decor.

The three sleeping rooms currently share a bathroom on the same floor, which has a shower and—for those who dare to weigh themselves—a scale. There is another bath on the main floor. The Smiths have plans to install additional bathrooms in the future.

After a long day of carriage rides, farm chores, or bicycle rides, you'll be glad to take a dip in the hot tub, where you can sit back, relax those muscles, and gaze at the stars. If it's hot and you need to cool off, you can head for the above-ground pool that shares the deck with the hot tub.

In addition to the bed and breakfast, the Smiths also offer package deals that include dinner and a carriage ride. Regardless, you'll find that the Smiths enjoy engaging in conversation with their guests and sharing the history of their farm. Whatever you choose to do during your stay at Our Country Home, this much is certain: you'll do it because you enjoy it, and you'll leave as a friend.

Biking from Our Country Home
The routes in the area pass over some gently rolling country, through woods, and near covered bridges. Crawfordsville itself is an attractive town with several diversions, including the Ben Hur Museum and the Lane Mansion. The very helpful Convention and Visitors Bureau, located right downtown, will provide you

with any information that you may need. If you have a penchant for Mexican food, a great place for lunch or dinner in town is the Little Mexico Restaurant.

An out-and-back route passes through pastoral scenery and eventually leads to the small village of Shanktown, renowned for its catfish. Visitors come from all over just to sample this tasty fish. The peaceful ride seems far removed from the hustle and bustle of daily living.

If you haven't had enough cycling after completing these routes, you can go to the Valley Bike Shop in town or the Montgomery County Convention and Visitors Bureau and pick up a booklet that contains several rides of various length that cross the county.

Terrain: The roads range from flat to undulating.

Road Conditions: The roads are in good condition and paved throughout.

Traffic: Very little out in the country, but traffic increases when approaching Crawfordsville.

Mountain Biking Opportunities: Ask for information at Valley Bike Shop.

Nearest Bike Shop
Valley Bike Shop
127 N. Washington Street
Crawfordsville, IN 47933
Phone: (765) 362-9615

Our Country Home to Darlington (34.3 miles)
Historic cemeteries, a covered bridge, and the picturesque town of Crawfordsville are the highlights of this trip. Be sure to take some time from the route to stroll the streets of pretty Crawfordsville and enjoy the architecture.

Cume	Turn	Street/Landmark
0.0	L	**550N** (from end of driveway)
1.0	R	**925E**
1.6	L	**SR 47**
3.7	R	**500N**
7.2	R	**400E**
7.9	L	**570N**
9.3	L	**550N**
10.2	L	**200E**
11.7	R	**400N**
12.8	L	**Concord Rd**.
15.4	L	**Highway 271**—*caution!*
17.6	L	**Wabash** (Goes through downtown area and near attractions)
18.9	R	**Main**
19.0	L	**Traction**
21.5	L	**400E**
22.0	R	**Highway 32**
22.1	L	**425E**
24.7	R	**Garfield**
25.5	BL	**300N**
26.7	L	**625E**
30.8	R	**400N**
32.3	L	**925E**
33.3	R	**550N**
34.3		Our Country Home

Our Country Home to Shanktown (22.2 miles, out and back)

Never at a loss for an appetite, bikers love to take a ride that has but one purpose: to satiate those pangs of hunger. This is one of those rides. People travel from miles away to enjoy the catfish dinners at Stookey's Family Dining. Pleasant pastoral scenery and low-traffic roads make this dining jaunt a pleasure.

0.0	L	**550N**
1.0	L	**925E**
2.5	L	**400N**

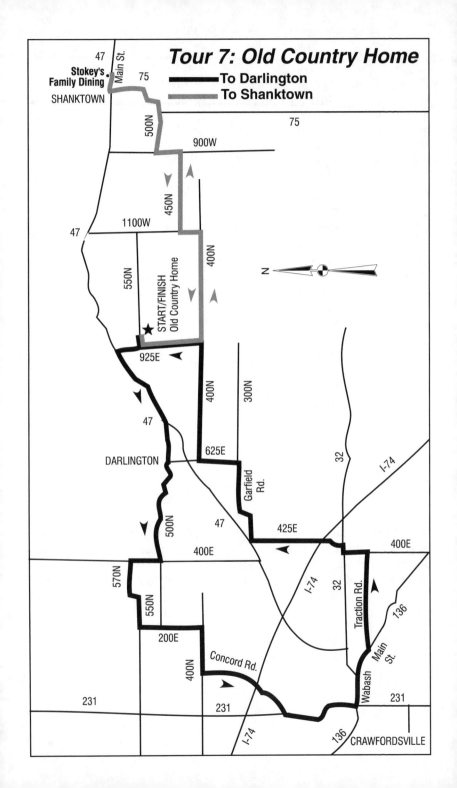

Cume	Turn	Street/Landmark
5.4	L	**1100W**
5.9	R	**450N**
7.9	L	**900W**
8.4	R	**500N**
9.5	L	**SR 75** (no sign)
10.9	R	**W. Main**
11.1	L	**Stookey's Family Dining**;
	TA	After filling up on catfish, turn around and retrace the route back to Our Country Home

The Schug House, Berne, Indiana

The Schug House Inn
706 West Main Street
Box 302
Berne, IN 46711
Phone: (219) 589-2303, (219) 589-2448
Innkeepers: John and Jane Minch
Rates: Budget

The chalet-style architecture that dots the quaint downtown area is an immediate tip-off to visitors that Berne, Indiana, was settled by the Swiss. The current residents are trying to keep that heritage alive, and have made Berne a delightful place to visit. A loudspeaker plays music for downtown strollers to enjoy, and Amish horse and buggies dot the streetscape.

Located on the main street of town, the Schug House Inn is a Queen Anne-style home with turrets and front porch. When John and Jane Minch purchased the home, they immediately started a year-long process of stripping paint, removing linoleum to expose the beautiful wood floors, and moving walls to improve traffic flow. The result of their labors will impress guests. Patterned hardwood floors, natural woodwork, and an attractive exterior give this hostelry an authentic feel. The Minches have installed private baths in all eight bedrooms and filled these comfortable spaces with a variety of antiques. The parlor in the front is tastefully decorated in warm antiques, making this a cozy area to relax or visit with other guests.

Two bedrooms are on the first floor. One—a small and cozy room that benefits from the morning sun—is decorated in shades of green and white with a floral wallpaper that is finished with a border. The lace-covered window lets the sun shine into this petite retreat. The second, a white and rose-colored room with a king-size bed (which can be separated into twins) has its own exit to the front porch where guests can sit and hope to catch a glimpse of a passing horse and buggy. The rocking chair perfectly complements the relaxing ambience of this pleasant room. The bathroom , a conversion from the back porch, has clapboard walls and a clawfoot tub and pedestal sink. Both first-floor rooms have an armoire, TV, and seating.

On the second floor, four rooms welcome guests. The first is set in the turret at the front of the house. A canopy covers the white and gold queen-size iron bed. The walls are salmon, with a subtle striped wallpaper embellished with nose-gays. A child's bed and a wicker table complete the furnishings.

Just across the hall, also in the turret, is another room with a queen-size bed with an oak headboard and a blue, white, and peach color scheme. With windows facing both the street and the side of the house, sun streams in throughout the day. Both of these turret rooms have ceiling fans.

To the rear of the house, you'll find one room that contains a queen bed, a lovely antique rocker, and a narrow fireplace mantel. Across the hall, another guestroom features a brass bed and another child-size bed. On the third floor, a huge area under the eaves accommodates families. The room can be divided so that parents can sleep separately from the children.

All of the bathrooms have a heater to warm you on chilly days or after riding in the rain. Some of the rooms have a ceiling fan; the whole house is air-conditioned.

If you need total privacy and seclusion, stay in the carriage house out back. This converted garage has a king bed that can be divided into two twins, a child's bed, and its own refrigerator stocked with beverages. Bicycles fit easily into these spacious quarters.

Back in the kitchen, which is manned by Amish servants, you'll find cold beverages waiting in the refrigerator. The Minches want you to feel at home and help yourself. If you or your group rents the entire house—as some people do—you may cook your own evening meals. For breakfast, you'll be served fruit, juice, tea or coffee, cereal, and fresh baked treats fresh from Mrs. Minch. There are three tables in the dining room to accommodate a full house of guests.

When planning your visit, keep in mind that Berne is one of those places where they roll up the carpets early, even on the weekends. But if you plan your visit around the Swiss Festival held the last weekend of July, be sure to make reservations far in advance.

By far, this bed and breakfast rates as one of the best values we've encountered. In fact, this was the first bed and breakfast that we enjoyed several years ago, and has served as a benchmark for all B&B visits.

Biking from The Schug House

Biking from the Schug house is on long, low-traffic roads through basically flat countryside. The first route passes old school houses, many of which are now converted to family homes, Amish farmsteads, and small towns. Near the pretty town of Bluffton, which has restaurants, antique shops, and interesting architecture, a bike path meanders along the Wabash River. A short detour outside of Bluffton leads to Oubache State Park.

Toward the end of the route, just on the outskirts of town, Swiss Heritage Village is an interesting stop that lets you explore some of the old, local-vernacular buildings that have been assembled on this site.

The second route heads basically in a southerly direction; you start out on what is known as the Amish highway, and you are likely to encounter horse and buggies along the way. While there are a significant number of Amish and Mennonites in the area, commercialism of their lifestyle has not taken hold here—you won't find cheesy gift shops or servers dressed as Amish women in restaurants. If you see somebody dressed in the Amish style, you can be sure that they are authentic practitioners of this lifestyle. This is not to say that you won't find places where you can learn about this interesting group of people: Just about a half mile off this route is Amishville, where you can visit a typical farmstead and eat Amish cuisine in an adjacent restaurant.

Just a short way from the turnoff, you will notice the old Ceylon Covered Bridge on the right hand side of the road. In the town of Geneva, Limberlost, one of the homes of author Gene Stratton Porter, is open to visitors. Besides the tour of the house, you may also like to take a self-guided tour of the area; maps are available at the house.

The next stop on the route is the round barn just before Fiet. At one time, farmers thought that this style of barn was a more practical and efficient way to feed the livestock. Few of these unique buildings remain today.

Furniture is a major industry in Berne, so be sure to take a tour of the Berne Furniture Factory, arranged through the chamber of commerce downtown.

Terrain: Flat.

Road Conditions: Good, with short hard-packed gravel stretches. Watch for wheel ruts in roads.

Traffic: Light except when approaching towns.

Nearest Bike Shop
Rick's Bike Shop
209 W. Jefferson
Decatur, IN
(219) 724-2705

Berne to Bluffton (35.2 miles)
This flat ride wanders along the Wabash River, eventually reaching the charming town of Bluffton. The park along the river is a perfect picnic spot. Berne has some good butchers to provide the makings for a packed lunch. Bluffton has some interesting buildings and all services.

Cume	Turn	Street/Landmark
0.0	L	**Main**
0.4	L	**CR 150**
1.4	R	**CR 700S**
5.0	L	**Linn**
5.2	R	**Second St.**
5.3	L	**Linn Grove**
5.9	S	**Rt. 116**
13.2	R	**450E**
13.6	L	**River Rd. Bike path** begins along river
15.7	-	Bike path ends
15.9	TA	**Main St.**
16.0	-	**River Greenway Bikepath** starts here along river
18.2	L	**450E**
18.5	R	**201**
18.9	L	**100S**
20.9	R	**700**
21.7	L	**Rt. 301**
22.7	L	**Church**
24.1	R	**200S**
26.1	R	**500W**
29.1	L	**500S**
31.1	L	**300W**
31.2	R	**500S**
33.2	-	*Caution:* cross US 27
33.7	R	**Swiss Way**
34.0	-	Swiss Village Entrance
34.2	R	**Parr**
34.3	L	**Sprunger**
34.9	R	**Main**
35.2	L	Schüg House

Round Barn Tour (37.2 miles)

Traversing back roads, you'll eventually reach an imposing presence on the horizon—a stately round barn. Indiana has the second-most round barns listed on the National Historic Register.

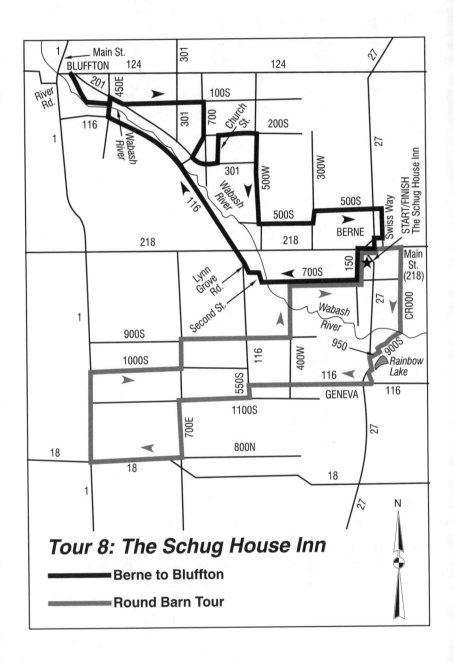

Tour 8: The Schug House Inn

▬▬▬ Berne to Bluffton

▬▬▬ Round Barn Tour

N

Cume	Turn	Street/Landmark
0.0	R	Main
1.1	R	CR000
4.0	R	CR 900S
5.2	L	Second
5.3	R	CR 950
5.4	L	Rainbow Lake
6.0	L	N. Railroad
6.5	R	Shackley
6.6	L	Decatur
6.8	R	Sixth
6.9	R	S. Main
7.1	L	SR 116
11.3	L	550W
11.8	R	1100S
14.4	L	700E
16.4	R	800N
16.5	R	SR 18
19.8	R	SR 1 (Restaurant)
21.8	R	1000S
25.1	L	700E
27.2	R	900S
31.2	L	400W
33.2	R	700S
35.8	L	150W
36.9	R	600S
37.2		Schug House

A home where the buffalo roam:
Wild Winds Buffalo Preserve, Fremont, Indiana

Wild Winds Buffalo Preserve

6975 Ray Clear Lake Road
Fremont, IN 46737
Phone: (219) 495-0137
Innkeeper: Ann Marie Wertz
Rates: Deluxe

"I, Chief Arvol Looking Horse of the Lakota Dakota and Nakota Nations look with great concern upon the continued slaughter of our relatives, the Buffalo Nation. According to the teachings for our way of life from the time of being, the First People were the Buffalo People; our ancestors that came from the sacred Black Hills, the heart of everything that is.

Our ceremonies consist of Seven Sacred Rites and with these rites we walk with the Buffalo Nation, not as lesser beings, but as our relatives. Only through them were we able to survive and we hold them in deep spiritual reverence and it is our inherent responsibility to protect them ... Their well-being is a reflection of the spiritual health of the people.

According to our prophecies, when there are no more buffalo, then life as we know it today will also cease to exist."

— Chief Arvol Looking Horse, 19th-Generation Sacred White Buffalo Calf Pipe Keeper

In the northeast corner of Indiana, a buffalo ranch thrives with over 600 head of Custer State Park bison. Although we commonly refer to these beasts as *buffalo*, the proper term is *American bison*. Whatever the name, preservation of the majestic and revered animal began with a smaller herd of six bison just across the border in Bryan, Ohio, before the owner purchased this 420-acre property.

A visit here will instill confidence that the future of the buffalo is in good hands. The property received the blessing of the Lakota

Sioux Indians, who often return to the preserve for spiritual ceremonies and to use parts of the buffalo—such as the skull—that are required for certain prescribed rituals. The connection between the tribe and the ranch necessitates a mutual respect among all parties. The brochure states that you should "come only of good spirit," for in Indian legend, the existence of this animal parallels the life and outlook for humans. In fact, the buffalo ranks just below The Great Spirit in terms of importance.

When we approached the preserve, we immediately noticed a pack of horses roaming the field. Because the ranch is so big, the buffaloes have plenty of room to roam and were not immediately visible. The thrill of seeing these honored beasts without having to drive thousands of miles to South Dakota makes a visit to Wild Winds a singularly amazing experience. To get a close up view of the buffalo, the ranch conducts organized tours in pickup trucks, which drive across the pastures. We happened to visit at calving time and viewed newborn calves just up on their wobbly feet. The public is welcomed to enjoy these tours on Sundays, although organized groups may visit by special arrangement at any time. But even with the crowds anxious to get a view of the buffalo, the preserve is a peaceful retreat.

With Ann Marie Wertz navigating the field, we learned much about the buffalo. In this particular herd, the females are boss. Each herd establishes its own hierarchy, and no two are alike. The male-female ratio favors the females, who prefer one male for every twelve females in this particular herd. The males are bigger and can be distinguished by their wider U-shaped horns. During calving season, the females assume a very protective role and may be tempted to charge if another human or buffalo is perceived as a threat.

This is the largest herd of Custer State Park buffalo outside of South Dakota. Ann Marie explained that, just like cows, buffaloes have different pedigrees. She is knowledgeable about the entire operation, probably because she is involved with everything that happens here on the ranch—and that means *every-*

thing. How she does it all and still maintains her energy is a wonder in itself. Ann Marie is also the innkeeper, the horse trainer, the herd manager and ... well, like we said, everything.

She explains that Wild Winds is meant to be a relaxing, if not spiritual, retreat. The guestrooms, found in a large log cabin and another smaller log building, all have exits to an exterior deck, where guests may sit and watch the buffalo roam. The large lodge brings to mind a typical western residence. High and open beamed ceilings create the illusion of a much larger space. Native artifacts grace the walls while a huge fireplace warms the room. Furniture made from ancient wood stands on the pine floors.

The guestrooms themselves are all similar. Wooden floors, knotty pine walls, and exposed beams create a cabin-like retreat. The bed frames are constructed of the same aged timber found in the other furnishings throughout the lodge. You are requested to pack your slippers, as the lodge is a shoe-fee environment. They are also handy for the short walk to the bathroom that two guestrooms share. Two other bedrooms that share a bath are located in a small lodge outside, and there are plans for additional guestrooms on the currently unfinished second level of the main lodge.

The most outstanding feature of the rooms is the buffalo skins, which cover the beds. Fortunately, you can order these wonderfully soft and comfortable accessories through the gift shop. Like the natives, Wild Winds uses the complete buffalo, so nothing is left to waste. In fact, as soon as they get approval from the state, they will be selling buffalo meat products at the gift shop on the premises.

A hearty breakfast can be served in the company of the ranch hands, or you can arrange to have a private meal. If you choose the former, you will certainly gain some insight into life on the ranch and the daily doings on the preserve. For a tour of the property, you may want to enjoy a trail ride, which Ann Marie is organizing along with the local unit of the Venture Scouts.

In the evening, your deck offers a perfect spot for stargazing or listening to the wildlife. Birds abound here, and other animals—such as the beaver—have moved onto the property.

Biking from Wild Winds Buffalo Preserve

Steuben County claims to have one hundred lakes, and attracts its share of tourists. The riding in the area traverses quiet lanes and rolling terrain. Lakes are scattered about the routes, but access to them for swimming or other activities seems limited. Clear Lake and Gage Lake are surrounded by seasonal cottages. Summer weekends—especially holiday weekends—might be a good time to avoid.

Terrain: Rolling hills with some flat areas.

Road Conditions: Roads are paved, but some have rough surfaces.

Traffic: Light for the most part, but heavier around Route 127. You should use extra caution on this well-traveled route, especially going through the shopping strip in Angola. During summer and holiday weekends, traffic may be annoying.

Nearest Bike Shop

Angola Schwinn
30 North Public Square
Angola, IN 46703-1924
Phone: (219) 665-8356

Wild Winds to Gage Lake (35.5 miles)

This route winds through some popular lake resort areas and even passes an amusement park. Be careful along North Wayne Street in Angola, which is also Route 127 (not to be confused with the North Wayne just outside of Fremont). Once beyond the shopping area, traffic decreases, but if you are uncomfortable riding in traffic, you could turn right on 200N and go back to Route 827 to return.

Cume	Turn	Street/Landmark
0.0	R	**Ray Clear Lake** (from the entrance of Wild Winds)
1.3	R	**Toledo (Rt. 120)**
1.5	L	**Rt. 827 (N. Wayne St.)**
6.4	R	**200N**
9.1	R	**200W**. _Caution:_ gravel shoulder, heavier traffic
9.6	L	**Orland**
10.0	BR	**Orland** (traffic increases)
14.2	BR	**Orland**
15.1	L	**Lake Gage**
15.8	BL	**Lage Gage** (rough road)
17.1	R	No sign
17.3	L	**350N**
18.4	R	**Orland**
19.7	R	**400W**
20.6	L	**Shady Side**
21.9	BR	**290**
22.6	L	**100N**
25.0	N	**Wayne St. (Rt. 127).** Heavy traffic, food right and left
29.1	R	**Feather Valley Rd.**
33.5	L	**Rt. 827**
34.0	R	**Toledo (Rt. 120)**
34.2	L	**Ray Clear Lake**
35.5		Wild Winds

Wild Winds to Clear Lake (20.4 miles)

This pleasant ride to Clear Lake has enough ups and downs to give you a workout—and it seems that mid-hill, the inclines become abruptly steeper. The advantage is, you'll get enough downward momentum to help conquer the next hill.

0.0	L	**Ray Clear Lake** (from entrance to Wild Winds)
0.7	BR	**750N**
4.7	R	**875E**
5.2	BL	**875E**
6.4	L	**850E**
6.9	L	**Rt. 120**

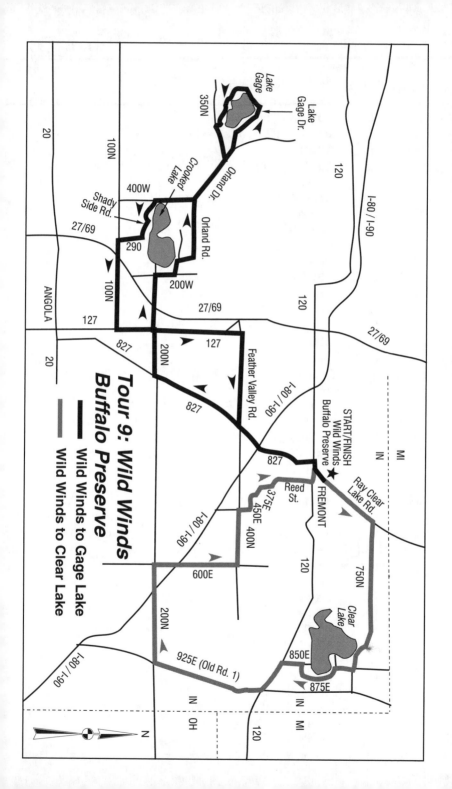

Tour 9: Wild Winds
Buffalo Preserve

Wild Winds to Gage Lake
Wild Winds to Clear Lake

Cume	Turn	Street/Landmark
7.7	R	**925E (Old Road 1)**
10.6	R	**200N**
13.0	R	**600E**
14.9	L	**400N**
16.4	R	**450E**, becomes **Peachy, 375E,** and **Reed**
18.9	L	**Rt. 120,** becomes **Toledo**
19.1	R/R	**Sierer**; take another immediate right to **Ray Clear Lake**
20.4		Wild Winds

Located in Jonesville, Michigan, the circa 1834 Munro House was once a stop on the Underground Railroad

Michigan

If you seek a pleasant peninsula, look about you.
— Michigan State Motto

The state of Michigan, with its Lower Peninsula shaped like a left-handed mitten, is known for its miles of shoreline on the Great Lakes, as well as its forests, rivers, and (relatively) smaller inland lakes. The listings in this section include only inns found on the Lower Peninsula; Michigan covers so much territory that the distance from Detroit to Copper Harbor is greater than the distance from Detroit to Washington, D.C.

Because water plays such an important role in the tourism industry in Michigan—and more importantly, since water seems to naturally attract visitors—every tour in this state will pass by a body of water, whether it be one of the Great Lakes, an inland lake, a river, or some combination of the above. The terrain in Michigan varies from relatively flat along the western shore and southern regions to very hilly in the Leelanau Peninsula.

Grass Lake includes parts of the Irish Hills, as well as the Waterloo Recreation Area and popular Clark Lake. The area around Sturgis boasts farm fresh markets, lakes, rivers, and a covered bridge. Small towns, Amish settlements, and wildlife areas abound in the Jonesville region. The town of White Lake lays claim to both an inland lake and takes advantage of its proximity to Lake Michigan; the nearby Hart Montague rail-trail and the gentle coastal terrain make this an ideal riding location for beginners.

Glenn occupies a convenient country location, making it easily accessible to Lake Michigan and the resort towns of South Haven and Saugatuck. Leland encompasses bits of everything: inland lakes, rivers and Lake Michigan as well as proximity to the Sleeping Bear Dunes National Park. Renowned for the Au Sable River and excellent canoeing, Grayling defines the true Northwoods experience.

No matter which area you choose, you'll have a great selection of bicycling adventures in Michigan's water wonderland.

Bed of Roses Bed & Breakfast, Howell, Michigan

Bed of Roses Bed & Breakfast

606 W. Grand River
Howell, MI 48843
Phone: (517) 545-1831
Web: www.bbonline.com/mi/bedofroses
Innkeeper: Patricia Jones
Rates: Budget

In the summer of 1863, a circus and menagerie, in combination, was exhibited at Howell, and while there one of the lions died. The showmen buried it on the old public square. In an early day, John W. Smith shot a grey eagle in this township, which measured over nine feet from tip to tip of its wings. Jesse Marr caught a pickerel with a spear, that weighed 21 pounds and 12 ounces. In the early settlement of the place, five elk were seen in the western part of the township. Two animals, known as Lynx, were caught in steel traps. Bears and wild cats were common game.

In the autumn of 1834, a wolf pursued a deer into the door-yard of David Austin. On the wolf's discovering the inmates of the house, it made its retreat, but the deer remained and was shot. In the fall of 1837, Henry Lake and his wife, with a young child, were returning from a neighbor's in the evening, and when within about thirty rods of their house, were attacked by wolves. One of them attempted to seize the child. It caught Mrs. Lake by her dress in making the effort but finally through the exertions of Mr. Lake and his dog, the animals were driven off. — 1868 History of Howell by Elisha Smith

In the heartland of Michigan, the town of Howell no longer remains the wild settlement that it once was, far removed from other settlements. Yet, in a way, it is still a remote town, its urban boundaries quickly melting into the rural landscape. The entire downtown area has been designated a National Historic District, not surprising since the area was one of the oldest settlements in the state. You can walk and explore the well-preserved village, with its interesting mix of old buildings and homes.

One of the century-old homes on Grand River Road, the main street that runs through town and stretches across this part of the state, is the Bed of Roses Bed and Breakfast. Once a road-house, the attractive white structure has also served as a lawyer's office and a Mental Health Services facility before becoming a wonderful bed and breakfast. Patricia Jones took on the project single-handedly and keeps an album showing the progress of the large home. Considerable renovation—much of it done by Patricia herself—has transformed the place into an elegant respite for travelers.

When you walk through the rear entrance you will be greeted by the cheerful Patricia, obviously (and justifiably) proud of this showplace. When the innkeeper puts her heart and soul into creating the perfect place, it is reflected in the enthusiastic hospitality that guests receive. Patricia welcomed us with a plate of fresh baked blueberry scones and hot tea. We sat around the table for hours and talked like long-lost friends, discussing our mutual home remodeling adventures.

Patricia continues to renovate and decorate more rooms for guests. The one room that is completed is located on the second floor, reached via a winding staircase. It contains a king-size bed with a cover that matches the drapes that Patricia made herself. A green wicker rocker and chair provide seating in the large and tastefully decorated room. An antique dresser and round stool fill out the room.

The walls are covered in a rich, deep-colored floral wallpaper, lending the room a regal air. The light pine floors are covered with an area rug to cushion your feet. The bathroom, complete with a Jacuzzi, is done in an elegant white tile. A fluffy terry robe is provided in the bedroom closet for the walk to the bathroom.

The other rooms all have natural wood floors. Having been given a preview of the fabrics to be used in the other rooms, it is clear that they will be equally attractive. The bedroom located on the first floor will have its own private bath.

Patricia takes a bold approach to decorating, but the effect is rather soothing. The living room, with the walls covered in a natural grasscloth wallpaper, offers cushy leather furniture for reading, watching the big-screen TV, or enjoying the warmth of the fireplace.

The dining room comes alive, awash in a tomato soup shade of red with a terra cotta hue on the cove molding. The effect instills a sense of calm and follows the theory that red stimulates the appetite—not that your appetite will need any stimulation after the aroma from the kitchen wafts through the rest of the house. Our tasty breakfast included a western-style omelette, stuffed full of red and green peppers, onions, chives, mushrooms, and cheese, accompanied by a nice fruit salad and toast.

The bed and breakfast is just a few blocks from the downtown area, a perfect distance for walking to dinner. Cleary's offers an extensive meal selection with something to please everyone, and is open for breakfast and dinner. Another popular eatery on the main drag is Mr. B's. Formerly a five-and-dime, the place brings back memories to people like Patricia, who remembers her children spending their savings on candy there.

For other information, Barb and Kathy at the Livingston County Convention and Visitors Bureau (located in the post office) can direct you to other points of interest in the county. One spectacular spot for mountain bikers is the Pinckney Recreation Area, which includes trails for both beginners and experts. For those looking for some paved bike trails, Kensington Metro Park is the place to go. Walking around the lake in town is another popular diversion that attracts walkers.

Biking from Bed of Roses

One particular characteristic of Livingston County—especially for cyclists—is the profusion of unpaved roads. One might get the idea that only the streets located within the village merit pavement; that guess would not be too far off base. Although you won't encounter wolves, lynx, or bears, you may still have a sense of being in the frontier. Michigan ranks high nationwide in the number of gravel roads existent throughout the state. For the cyclist, that means that a good percentage of the roads on this route are unpaved. However, they are hard-packed and offer the advantage of not having a significant amount of traffic. On the other hand, it also means that the paved roads you _do_ ride on will carry a bit more traffic.

While following these routes, you'll witness pastoral landscapes and large crop farms. With the increase in suburban housing developments pushing into rural areas and destroying land that provides food and grain, it is refreshing to have a chance to see that this type of land still exists. The first route follows meandering rural roads through small villages and desolate farmland. The second passes the Pinckney Recreation Area, an outdoor adventurer's paradise, where the terrain rolls through forest and farmland.

Terrain: Ranges from relatively flat to hilly.

Road Conditions: Lots of hard packed gravel.

Traffic: Heavier along the paved roads, very little on gravel.

Mountain Biking Opportunities: The Pinckney Recreation Area offers excellent mountain biking for all skill levels.

Nearest Bike Shop
Town & Country Cyclery
8160 Grand River Road
Brighton, MI 48114-9376
Phone: (810) 227-4420

Country Ramble (36.6 miles)

Cume	Turn	Street/Landmark
0.0	R	**Grand River Rd.**
0.1	R	**Byron Rd.**
5.8	R	**Allen** (hardpacked gravel)
7.1	L	**Oak Grove Rd.**
7.8	L	**Oak Grove Rd.**

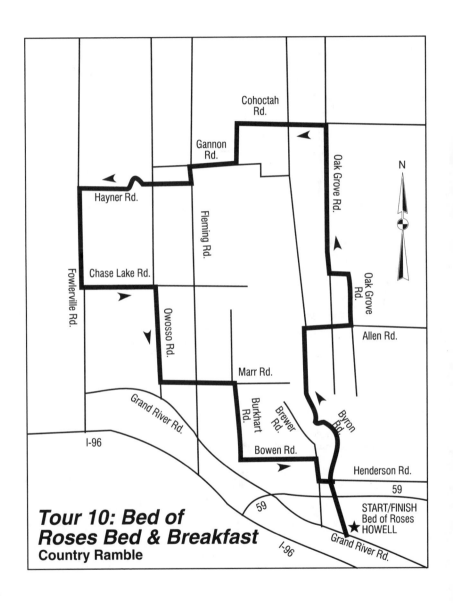

Cohoctah Rd.

Gannon Rd.

N

Hayner Rd.

Oak Grove Rd.

Fleming Rd.

Chase Lake Rd.

Oak Grove Rd.

Fowlerville Rd.

Owosso Rd.

Allen Rd.

Marr Rd.

Grand River Rd.

Burkhart Rd.

Brewer Rd.

Byron Rd.

I-96

Bowen Rd.

Henderson Rd.

59

START/FINISH
Bed of Roses
HOWELL

59

Tour 10: Bed of Roses Bed & Breakfast
Country Ramble

I-96

Grand River Rd.

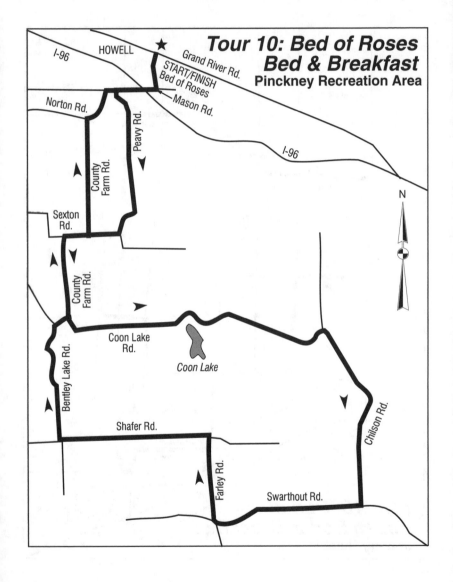

Tour 10: Bed of Roses Bed & Breakfast
Pinckney Recreation Area

I-96
HOWELL
Grand River Rd.
START/FINISH
Bed of Roses
Mason Rd.
Norton Rd.
Peavy Rd.
County Farm Rd.
I-96
Sexton Rd.
County Farm Rd.
Bentley Lake Rd.
Coon Lake Rd.
Coon Lake
Shafer Rd.
Chilson Rd.
Farley Rd.
Swarthout Rd.
N

Cume	Turn	Street/Landmark
12.7	L	**Cohoctah Rd.**
15.9	BR	**Gannon Rd.**
17.1	BL	**Fleming**
17.6	BR	**Hayner**
20.7	L	**Fowlerville Rd.**
23.3	L	**Chase Lake Rd.**
25.3	R	**Owosso Rd.**
27.7	L	**Marr**
29.8	R	**Burkhart Rd.**
31.8	L	**Bowen Rd.**
33.8	R	**Brewer Rd.**
34.3	L	**Henderson Rd.**
34.8	R	**Byron Rd.**
36.2	L	**W. Clinton**
36.4	R	**West St.**
36.5	R	**W. Grand River**
36.6	R	Bed Of Roses

Pinckney Recreation Area (32.9 miles)

Cume	Turn	Street/Landmark
0.0	L	Along **sidewalk**
0.1	S	Cross Grand River to **Jewett**
0.3	R	**Maple St.**
0.5	L	**Isbell**
0.8	R	**Mason**
1.3	L	**Peavy**
4.1	R	**Sexton**
5.1	S	**County Farm**
5.2	BL	**County Farm**
6.8	L	**Coon Lake**
8.8	S	*Caution* crossing D 19
12.3	R	**Chilson**
15.8	R	**Swarthout**
18.7	R	**Farley**
20.3	L	**Shafer**
21.0		*Caution* crossing D19; party store, pizza, gas station
23.1	R	**Bentley Lake**

Cume	Turn	Street/Landmark
25.4	R	Coon Lake
25.7	L	County Farm
27.2	BR	Sexton
27.3	BL	County Farm
29.4	BR	Norton
30.3	BR	Mason
31.1	R	Isbell
32.0	R	Pine Hill Apartments
32.3	L	Walnut
32.5	L	Maple
32.6	R	Jewett
32.8	L	Grand River
32.9	R	Bed of Roses

Borchers Bed & Breakfast

101 Maple Street
Grayling, MI 49738
Phone: (517) 348-4921, (800) 762-8756
Fax: (517) 348-2986
E-mail: chunter@borchers.com
Web: www.borchers.com/bb.html
Innkeepers: Mark and Cheri Hunter
Rates: Budget

> *Nothing is more beautiful than the loveliness*
> *of the woods before sunrise.*
> — George Washington Carver

Away from the big city, Grayling offers a small town experience with nature at its doorstep. Here in the northern part of Michigan's lower peninsula, you can really have it all. The woods cover much of the area, demonstrating why the region earned its livelihood on the logging industry. The Au Sable River, which flows to Lake Huron, peacefully meanders through town. State lands abound and lakes dot the landscape. The scents emanating from the forest delight the olfactories, and the peacefulness of the woods soothes the nerves.

Nearby Hartwick Pines State Park exhibits a history of the logging days along with other interpretive displays. Hiking and mountain biking trails wind through the park. North Higgins Lake State Park boasts a sparkling blue lake, beckoning the cyclist for a dip about midway on the second biking route below. The campfire smoke drifting through the air resurrected thoughts of childhood camping trips to this great park, roasting marshmallows in the evening. The urge to pitch a tent eventually subsided as the priorities for this particular trip triumphed.

Situated on the banks of the Au Sable, Borchers Bed and Breakfast offers not only a comfortable place to stay but also serves as a base for canoe trips on the river. Cheri and Mark Hunter pride themselves on preserving the river for future generations. Along with other liveries on the Au Sable, they have enlisted the aid of local marine deputy agencies to ensure that canoeists have a peaceful, safe, and enjoyable day on the river—no glass, radios, or excessive alcohol are permitted. Like the silent sport of cycling, canoeing lets you use your senses to enjoy the subtleties of nature. If you happen to be in the area on the last full weekend in July, you'll be able to watch the canoe race on the Au Sable that begins with a mass start in Grayling and follows the river's length all the way to Lake Huron. The upstairs balcony, in the comfort of a wicker chair, is the perfect place to watch this feat of endurance, considered by some to be more difficult than the Iditarod. Should you happen to be in the area when the conditions are more suitable for an Iditarod, be aware that cross-country skiing, alpine skiing, snow shoeing and snowmobiling are popular in the area.

A large colonial structure with six guestrooms, Borchers is a very informal and relaxing place with the atmosphere of a vacation home or lodge. Several guests admonished us for working during our stay, reminding us that this was a place for vacation. In spite of all the work that Mark and Cheri do, they still find time to chat with the guests and make them feel at home. Mark gladly shared his experiences in maintaining the scenic quality of the Au Sable River.

For visiting with other guests, the living room has several sofas and a table where you might engage in a game of cards or a board game. For the musically inclined, a string bass leans against the living room wall—be sure to get the story behind this massive instrument. A television, VCR, and a selection of movies are also found in this common room.

All guestrooms are located on the second floor, with half having private baths and half having air-conditioning; it isn't necessarily the same rooms that have both. Since the inn was full during our visit, we were not able to see most of the rooms. Those we did see seemed to follow a common cottage-cozy style. Several of the upstairs rooms have a paneled wainscoting complemented by wallpaper. Our room was done in pink with a floral border, a pink chair, and a corner shelf with knickknacks and a TV. A small private bath contained a shower. An off-white plush carpet padded the floor while a ceiling fan supplemented the window air conditioner. The queen-sized bed claimed a significant share of the room, which was arranged for maximum comfort.

The dining room is decorated in a homespun theme, with a fireplace and a large country-style table and chairs that can accommodate all of the guests when they're around (during our stay, the other guests spent most of their time away from the inn, taking advantage of the multitude of activities available in the surrounding area). Our breakfast consisted of fresh fruit, juice, Borchers breakfast pie, mini-cinnamon rolls, tea and coffee, cereal, and ham—great fuel for a day of pedaling and paddling.

Porches on both the upper and lower level offer the perfect place to take it easy and watch the river and canoeists pass by. Outside of the house there are picnic tables and benches, even a firepit if you have the inclination to barbecue your own dinner.

For a restaurant dinner, try Steven's in downtown Grayling, a short walk from Borchers. It has reasonably priced foods in an atmosphere straight out of the diner in *Happy Days*. They make an excellent mulligatawny stew, but the big draw is the variety of ice cream concoctions—anything from a cone to a giant sundae.

Biking from Borchers

Terrain: Mostly gentle, with some rolling hills.

Road Conditions: Some roads are rough, and a few are hard-packed gravel.

Traffic: Generally light until you arrive back in town. The intersection of M-72 and Business I-75 requires caution.

Mountain Biking Opportunities: Hartwick Pines State Park and Hanson Hills.

Nearest Bike Shop
The Bicycle Shop
200 E. Michigan
Grayling, MI 49738
Phone: (517) 348-6868

Grayling to Higgins Lake (29.2 miles)

Cume	Turn	Street/Landmark
0.0	R	**Maple**
0.2	L	**Dale**
0.3	R	**Lawndale**
0.4	L	**Huron**
2.0	R	**Barker Lake Rd.** (gravel)
6.2	R	**4 Mile Rd.**
8.6	L	**Old 27** (also called **South Grayling** or **Crawford County 27**)
15.8	R	**North Higgins** (state park is to the left)
16.2	R	Stop sign (road unmarked, sign says "To Camp Grayling")
24.8	R	**Rt. 93** (sign says "To Grayling")
27.0	R	**M-72**
28.4	S	Get into center lane to go straight
28.6	R	**Maple**
29.2	R	Borchers entry

Grayling to Hartwick Pines (out and back—15 miles)
Although this is a short ride, you will find that you could spend a good part of the day exploring Hartwick Pines. The mountain biking loops through the forest are not difficult and offer several distance options.

0.0	L	**Maple**
0.2	R	**Michigan**
0.5		Jog left at curve
0.8	R	**N. Down River**
2.5	L	**Wilcox Bridge** (some gravel stretches)
5.1	R	**93N** (Wilcox Bridge ends here)

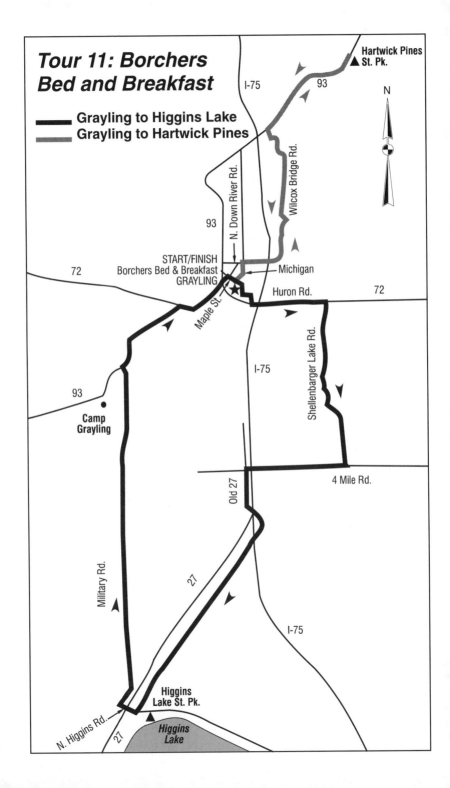

Tour 11: Borchers Bed and Breakfast

━━━━ Grayling to Higgins Lake
▨▨▨ Grayling to Hartwick Pines

Hartwick Pines
▲ St. Pk.

N

I-75

93

Wilcox Bridge Rd.

N. Down River Rd.

93

72

START/FINISH
Borchers Bed & Breakfast
GRAYLING

Michigan

Huron Rd.

72

Maple St.

Shellenbarger Lake Rd.

93

Camp
Grayling

I-75

I-75

4 Mile Rd.

Old 27

Military Rd.

27

Higgins
Lake St. Pk.

N. Higgins Rd.

27

Higgins
Lake

Cume	Turn	Street/Landmark
6.8	L	**Hartwick Pines** entrance
7.1	R	Follow sign to visitor center
7.5	TA	**Visitor center**
7.9	L	Follow exit signs
8.2	R	**93N**
9.9	L	**Wilcox Bridge**
12.5	R	**N. Down River**
14.2	L	**Michigan**
14.8	L	**Maple**
15.0	R	Borchers

Christmere House Inn

110 Pleasant Street
Sturgis, MI 49091
Phone: (888) 651-8303
Fax: (616) 659-5900
E-mail: christmere@rivercountry.com
Web: www.rivercountry.com/christmere
Innkeeper: Janette Parr Johns
Rates: Budget to Deluxe

"I do think people who love old houses love to share."
— Jan Johns, Innkeeper

Jan Johns welcomed us with open arms on a sweltering day and shared with us the history of Christmere House Inn and her warm, generous hospitality. It is no wonder that the Christmere House was full on this day—repeat guests and word of mouth contribute to the popularity of this Queen Anne home, built in 1882.

Originally, the home was designed by architects upon the request of a local doctor. He wanted the house to function as both a family home and a community hospital. The building served this role until 1928, when it became a rooming house. When Jan rescued the dilapidated structure from the wrecking ball in 1984, she was one of only a handful of townspeople who recognized the potential for the deteriorating gem and was undeterred by the huge amount of work and money needed to get this queen back on her throne. With the help of her son-in-law, she started a new project. Guests now enjoy this grand mansion without any hint of its past misery.

Jan expends plenty of energy attending to the inn and working on other projects. Besides her role as an innkeeper, she is a writer, publisher, and consultant for other innkeepers. One of the books that Jan has published is a guide to bed and breakfasts in the Great Lakes states; you can pick up a free copy at the inn or at the state tourism bureau. She commits a great deal of time and effort to promoting the non-coastal areas of Michigan, including the area around Sturgis. Fortunately, the local tourism association proactively promotes the area with the same goals in mind as Jan. Rivers, forests, fresh fruit markets, and an interesting covered bridge wait to be discovered by visitors to the area.

One of Jan's many previous jobs included managing a country club. Today, Jan continues in that vein, serving dinner at the Christmere house. Her meals get rave reviews, but because of the excessive heat when we were there, she decided to close the kitchen for a few evenings. A typical menu might consist of the following entrees: New York strip, crab stuffed shrimp, orange roughy on a bed of crabmeat, lamb chops with mint jelly, or chicken royal. During our visit, she was enclosing an area of the porch so that dinner guests could enjoy the outdoors while giving her the capacity to accommodate more diners.

As Jan points out, she is the best place in town for a meal, but she did recommend the next closest place for dining out, which was quite a drive away. But the setting on the shores of Fisher Lake near Three Rivers made the drive worthwhile. Unfortunately, the popularity of this eatery required us to wait longer that we would have liked. Like the concerned innkeeper she is, Jan became a bit anxious when it got late and we had not yet returned.

The morning feast served by Jan will please the pickiest eater. She serves just the right amount of food with just the perfect amount of seasoning—don't expect an ordinary breakfast here. The lovely dining room setting, with deep woods, a reddish carpet, and cloth-covered tables, encourages guests to relax and converse well beyond typical breakfast hours. Several hours pass quickly by when in the presence of good company and comfortable surroundings.

After passing a splendid night in the very comfy Queens Tower Suite, we felt like royalty. Perched up on the third floor, we marveled at the architecture of the ceiling, while the sense of being under massive naves added a feeling of vastness to this space.

And the room does cover a lot of area—besides the sleeping quarters, there is a mini-kitchen with a refrigerator and microwave. The bath has antique fixtures, and under the eaves on one side of the room is a wonderful whirlpool tub that defines the real meaning of "bathroom." The Queen Ann-style furnishings add to the feeling of charm and elegance. Daybeds for relaxation, reading material, a ceiling fan ... what more could one want for indulgence? This self-contained retreat tempts even the most gung-ho cyclist to just relax and enjoy the surroundings.

St. Joseph County, Michigan, claims the largest number of navigable bodies of water in Michigan. Canoeing is a popular activity, but other diversions include the Langley Covered Bridge (the longest in Michigan) just north of Centreville, the Magic Capital of Colon, and the nearby Amish country in neighboring Indiana. Kelley Lamb, the director of River Country Tourism, will provide you with enough diversions to keep you in St. Joseph County for a week or more. She and Jan both do a wonderful job of selling their county and accommodating guests.

If you visit the Christmere House web page, you might notice that this lovely inn is for sale. Maybe after talking to Jan, you'll be so enthused about the prospect of being an innkeeper that you consider becoming the new owner. While Jan loves her innkeeping responsibilities, she also looks forward to retirement. Whoever takes over as innkeeper at the Christmere House will have a great mentor from whom to learn.

Biking from The Christmere House
The terrain in these parts is gentle, and if you really want to get in a lot of bicycling miles, you have a choice of twelve different routes that meander throughout the countryside. The routes can be found both on the internet and through the River Country Convention and Visitors Bureau.

Terrain: Mostly flat with the occasional hill.

Road Conditions: Good, mostly paved roads, with short stretches of hard-packed gravel.

Traffic: Light to moderate.

Nearest Bike Shop
The Kickstand Schwinn
1240 E. Chicago
Sturgis, MI 49091
Phone: (616) 651-5088

Christmere House to the Lakelands (29.3 miles)
This enjoyable route traverses shaded roads and lots of small lakes visible through the trees. You'll pass several fruit stands, so stop and indulge yourself. There are parks with picnic tables in the small towns. The terrain is not too demanding, with just the occasional rolling hills.

Cume	Turn	Street/Landmark
0.0	L	**Pleasant**
0.1	L	**W. Congress**
0.2	R	**S. Nottawa** (brick road)
1.2	L	**W. Fawn River**
5.2	L	**Fawn River** (gravel)
5.7	BR	**Fawn River**
6.7	L	**Halfway** (pavement begins)
10.6	R	**W. Front**
10.8	L	**S. Second**
11.0	L	**Main**
11.2	R	**5th**
11.5	L	**3rd**
11.9	R	**Middle Colon**
13.7	L	**Hackman**
14.1	R	**Findley**
19.4	S	*Caution*, cross Rt. 55
20.5	L	**Nottawa**
22.5	L	**Banker**
23.2	R	**Bogert**
23.6	R	**Rommel**
24.6	R	**Featherstone**
24.8	L	**N. Centreville**
28.5	L	**West**

Cume	Turn	Street/Landmark
29.0	**R**	**N. Nottawa**
29.1	**R**	**E. Chicago**
29.2	**L**	**Pleasant**
29.3		Christmere House

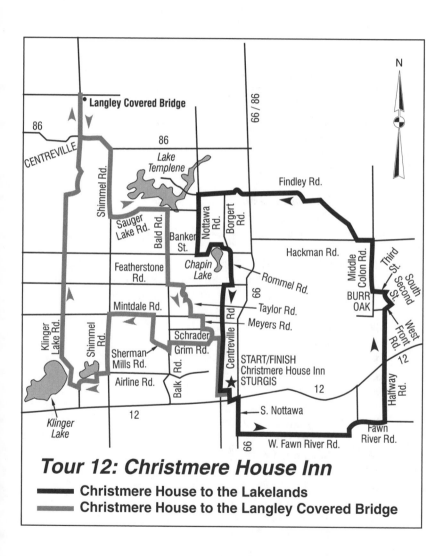

Tour 12: Christmere House Inn

━━━━ **Christmere House to the Lakelands**

▬▬▬ **Christmere House to the Langley Covered Bridge**

Christmere House to the Langley Covered Bridge (34.7 miles)
The beautiful, bright red—and, at 282 feet, very long—covered bridge is definitely worth the short detour from the route and is a highlight of this trip. Centreville itself is a pleasant town. The terrain is mostly flat with a few minor rises, but you should watch for loose gravel and buggies along the way. There is a very nice park on the other side of the bridge. *Note:* Start this ride by crossing the parking lot next to Christmere and starting at the street behind the inn.

Cume	Turn	Street/Landmark
0.0	R	Through **parking lot**
0.1	L	**S. Nottawa**
1.9	L	**Wait**
2.4	R	**Centreville**
2.6	L	**Schrader**
3.0	L	**Grim**
4.7	L	**Balk**
4.8	R	**Sherman Mills**
6.3	L	**Mintdale**
7.8	L	**Shimmel**
9.9	R	**Airline**
11.3	R	**Klinger Lake**
20.4	-	Continue straight for 3.1 miles to the **covered bridge**, then retrace back to this point
20.4	R	**M-86**
21.6	R	**Shimmel**
23.9	L	**Sauger Lake**
25.9	R	**Balk**
28.5	L	**Featherstone**
29.0	R	**Taylor**
30.2	L	**Mintdale**
30.7	R	**Meyers**
31.2	L	**Schrader**
32.1	R	**Centreville**
34.0	L	**West**
34.3	R	**Clay**
34.5	L	**W. Chicago**
34.6	R	**Pleasant**
34.7		Christmere House

Coppys Inn

13424 Phal Road
Grass Lake, MI 49240
Phone: (517) 522-4850
Web: www.getaway2smi.com/coppys/index.htm
Innkeepers: Willy and Sharon Coppernoll
Rates: Budget to Moderate

The happiest conversation is that of which nothing is distinctly remembered, but a general effect of pleasing impression.—Samuel Johnson

On the outskirts of the small community of Grass Lake stands a farmstead that has been in the same family for nearly a century. Set on 65 acres, Coppys Inn offers a pleasant atmosphere for relaxation and reinvigoration. When you walk in the front door after a warm greeting from Sharon Coppernoll, you immediately notice the large commercial stove that dominates the kitchen. But your gaze immediately focuses on the multicolored walls tinted in the bright and bold hues of raspberry, maize, and deep green. Sharon consulted a decorator for color suggestions that would bring life to the formerly all-white walls. Hesistant at first about using such a shocking palette, she heeded the advice of her painter, who said that the decorator's colors—although appearing outrageous at first—always go together well and create a wonderful ambience. These strong shades highlight a beautiful quilt that hangs against the raspberry wall, illuminating the yellow sections of the quilt.

Throughout the inn, a country theme dominates, although it is not excessive or repetitive. Just the right amounts of accessories and color account for the soothing effect that guests will notice in each of the rooms. On the first floor a large space provides several seating areas for mingling with other guests, reading, playing games, or watching TV. Comfortable furniture in an assortment of styles invites guests to sit and enjoy themselves. On an enclosed front porch reached through French doors, a light and airy breakfast room is the sun-drenched spot for breakfast. Several tables accommodate guests in perfect conversational groupings. Birds and birdhouses throughout the area bring the outdoors inside.

We enjoyed a scrumptious breakfast of stuffed French toast, one of Sharon's many specialties. Having grown up in the restaurant business, cooking comes easily to Sharon, as evidenced by her delicious menus and her ability to efficiently serve groups of up to 40 people. Sharon will gladly recommend other establishments for your dining pleasure. For a good home-cooked meal, try the café on the main street in Grass Lake, which offers large servings at reasonable prices.

Guests have their choice of seven bedrooms at Coppys, all but one of which are located on the second floor. On the first floor, The Homestead Room pays tribute to Willy Coppernoll's ancestors, who settled the farm in the early 1900s. The old oak bed belonged to Willy's grandfather, and an old clawfoot soaking tub in the private bath provides the opportunity for rest and relaxation.

Reached via a grand staircase, the second-floor bedrooms center around a wide hall. In a new addition to the inn, The Loft is a two-bedroom suite that offers flexible options for guests. The large room is a very private and comfortable retreat with a whirlpool tub, television, and a queen bed within its confines. Separated from the rest of the house by a hallway with automatic lights, this main room occupies one end of the house. The cathedral ceilings give this space an air of grandeur while the neutral tones of the wallpaper provide a subtly elegant effect. Carpeted through-out, the room has plenty of space to stretch out and enjoy a beverage—or breakfast in bed, if you so desire. Fluffy robes hang in the room for your convenience to use after a dip in the tub or on the walk to the bathroom, which is just outside the door and is shared with the neighboring room.

The second room in the suite consists of two twin beds that can be converted into a king-size bed if so desired. Set under the eaves, the blue-grey sponged ceiling adds dramatic detail to the room. The walls are done in a pattern that resembles leopard skin, but in a sage-blue color. If somebody has rented the larger room, the twin room will not be rented to strangers. The cycling groups that stay here take up the whole house and don't mind sharing. But if you have reserved this room for a special occasion, you need not worry about having to share the bathroom or the area with other guests. Another nice feature in The Loft is the separate coffee maker for occupants of this room.

Back at the other end of the house, the next room that you will come to is Sue Ellen, decorated much in the manner of a sophisticated young girl's room. The color scheme adds a delicate air to the room, as do the pleated blinds, white Priscilla curtains, and porcelain doll. The space is enlarged by the beamed cathedral ceiling. A dress and straw hat, needlepoint portraits, and quilted pieces grace the walls. The antique walnut double bed fits snugly in an alcove. Light hardwood floors are covered by throw rugs scattered about the room. The bathroom, which contains a shower, pays tribute to the younger child with framed illustrations of a youngster's toileting adventures. Cotton robes are provided for your comfort, both here and in the remaining rooms.

Next door to Sue Ellen, The Eyry of the Eagle mixes styles and colors that show a slightly masculine leaning. The unobtrusive combination of copper, taupe, and dark green colors give this room a very dignified air. Like Sue Ellen, it has a cathedral ceiling with exposed beams. Decorating the walls are snapshots taken by a local helicopter photographer. An electric fireplace adds a cozy element that will warm you when you crawl out of the king-size bed. There is also a private bath.

Around the corner, the Ted E. Bear room celebrates an American tradition. Red, white, and blue add a splash of color to this whimsical room. The valences have teddy bears on them and a group of the cuddly beasts in a variety of forms watches over the headboard of the antique white cast iron bed. The room is small, but what it lacks in space, it makes up for in charm. The private bath has a tub/shower combination and, of course, more teddy bears spread about.

Amelias's Room is located at the end of the hall. The large room will please those who love the color purple; the dominant hue is complemented with dark green. A beautiful wall hanging, a similarly colored quilt and a watercolor named "Amelia's Quilt" complete the décor. A desk and chair for writing and another table and chairs for sipping coffee mean there is plenty of space to spread out.

Biking from Coppys

The countryside around the farm offers ideal cycling routes, one of which visits Clark's Lake and passes by several other small lakes. Known as the Irish Hills because the first settlers thought the area resembled their homeland, the rolling terrain adds interest to the route. The town of Brooklyn, just a short detour off the route, has full services, antique shops, and other diversions. Michigan International Speedway is nearby, and during race weekends—occurring one weekend in June, July, and August—cycling is not recommended because the traffic is horrendous.

The second route passes through the Waterloo Recreation Area. Take a rest and observe the wildlife or just stop for a picnic along the way. Wetlands and natural areas abound, while tunnels of trees cloak the roads in verdant shade. Back in the town of Grass Lake, there is a lake of the same name. Nearby, a group of Italian priests is renovating a barn into a shrine surrounded by meditation gardens. The well-thought-out renovation is very visually pleasing; when the shrine is completed, it will surely attract many visitors.

Other nearby points of interest include the Jackson Space Center, Sharon Winery, Purple Rose Theater, and the Waterloo Farm Museum.

Terrain: Flat to rolling, especially in the Irish Hills area.

Road Conditions: Very good. Jackson County has well-marked roads with marked warning signs before each approaching road. The best county road system yet!

Traffic: Generally light, but be sure to avoid Michigan International Speedway weekends.

Nearest Bike Shop
On 2 Wheels
550 Laurence
Jackson, MI
Phone: (517) 789-6077

Coppys to The Lakes (32.7 miles)
Several resort lakes dot the map in the area and this route passes by a few of them. Stop and eat at a restaurant in Clark's Lake or take some time and explore the streets of historic Brooklyn. Bring a swimsuit if you want to take a plunge into one of the lakes along the way.

Cume	Turn	Street/Landmark
0.0	R	**Phal Rd.**
1.5	L	**Norvell**
1.6	R	**Phal Rd.**
3.2	L	**Wolf Lake**
5.2	R	**Rexford**
6.7	-	Road changes name to **Oak Point Rd.**
7.9	R	**Cady**
8.8	L	**Napoleon**
9.3	-	*Caution* crossing M 50
9.9	R	**Stony Lake Rd.**
13.3	L	**Clark Lake Rd.**
16.0	L	**North Lake Rd.**
16.8	R	**Ocean Beach Rd.**
17.4	L	**Riverside**
20.2	R	**Brooklyn (M 50)**
20.5	L	**Case Rd.**
20.7	BL	**Case**
22.8	BL	**Case**
26.4	L	**Mill**
26.6	L	**Commercial Rd.**
26.8	-	Road changes name to **Norvell**
31.2	R	**Phal Rd.**
32.7	L	Coppys

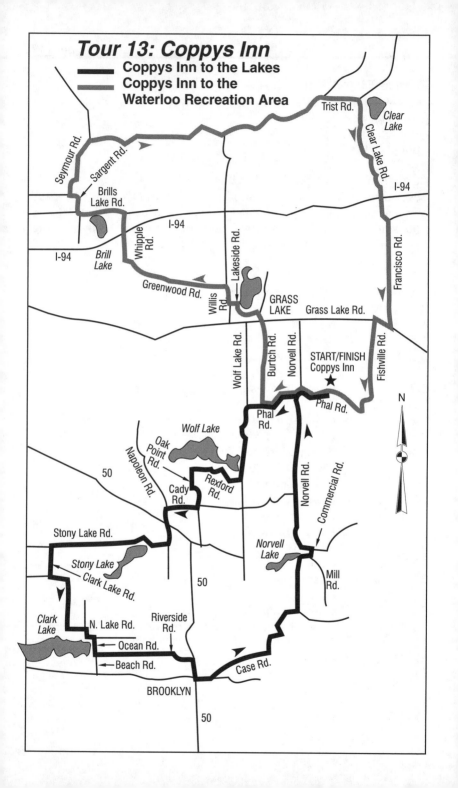

Coppys to the Waterloo Recreation (33.3 miles)

Passing through the village of Grass Lake will start this adventure into the wonderful Waterloo Recreation Area. Wildlife viewing areas are located along this route through shady forests and wetland areas.

Cume	Turn	Street/Landmark
0.0	R	**Phal Rd.**
1.5	L	**Norvell**
1.6	R	**Phal Rd.**
2.7	R	**Burtch**
5.4	L	**Lakeside**
6.3	R	**Willis**
6.8	L	**Greenwood**
9.8	R	**Whipple**
11.2	L	**Brills Lake Rd.**
12.4	R	**Sargent Rd.**
13.2	R	**Seymour Ave.**
19.2	-	Little Restaurant
21.8	BR	Main road changes name to **Trist**
23.0	R	**Clear Lake Rd.**
26.6	BR	**Francisco Rd.**
29.6	R	**Grass Lake Rd.**
30.1	L	**Fishville Rd.**
32.9	R	**Phal Rd.**
33.3	R	Driveway of inn

Manitou Manor, Leland, Michigan

Manitou Manor

147 North Manitou Trail West
P.O. Box 864
Leland, MI 49654
Phone: (231) 256-7712
Innkeepers: Sandy and Mike Lambdin
Rates: Budget to Moderate

"Si quaeris peninsulam amoenam, circumspice." — *"If you seek a pleasant peninsula, look about you."* — Michigan State Motto

Flecked with scenic lakes, the Leelanau Peninsula points out like a dainty little finger into Lake Michigan. Small and reserved resort towns, like Northport, Leland, Suttons Bay, and Glen Arbor entice visitors with their proximity to the water. Much of the area is included in the Sleeping Bear Dunes National Lakeshore, a unit of the National Park Service.

Mike and Sandy Lambdin left behind the hustle and bustle of business life to find a retirement activity they would love. Welcoming guests at the Manitou Manor, a large farmhouse with an interesting past, has become their vocation. Once a one-story house located on the opposite side of the street, for years it was known as the Lattice Lodge, a tearoom that catered to travelers. At another time it housed the elderly. It was transformed into a bed and breakfast before being purchased by Mike and Sandy. They have added their own personal flair, which is so well received that the participants in a commercial bicycle tour rated it their favorite place to stay on a tour. It is pitch black at night, making it great for sleeping and also stargazing.

Mike is in seventh heaven planting a new hedge full of an amazing number and variety of plants. Some of these colorful specimens have been acquired through a plant exchange program that Sandy and Mike encourage. A friend once brought in 100 plants—which made no dent in the project whatsoever. The scope is truly amazing and the outcome will be impressive.

All rooms at Manitou Manor have names that start with the letter I. Infante, where we stayed, has some little dolls, cherubs, and a Cabbage Patch in a highchair. The queen-size bed was unique in that the footboard was suspended from the ceiling to make a canopy. The huge closet converts into a child's private quarters, a place that younger and smaller guests will enjoy.

Interlude caters to honeymooners and others seeking a romantic sojourn. The king-size bed is covered with a lace and floral canopy. Wedding-related items, such as a veil and other delicate accessories, grace the room.

Indiana suggests a more masculine space, with deep, rich colors with wildlife influences. Ducks and fish border the room, which also contains bedside tables made from barrels and a pharmacists desk.

True to its name, Indigo displays bursts of this color in the patch quilt on the bed, and is contrasted with light blue, pink, and white. An interesting rolled fabric border skirts the ceiling.

Inverness replicates a garden. The bed, with its unique wrought iron headboard, snuggles into an alcove. Stars cover the ceiling, imitating the night sky.

All guestrooms have private baths with hand-held showers, a wonderful accessory for soothing muscles after a bike ride. In keeping with the inn's location in the heart of Michigan's wine country (one winery is right across the street), wine glasses are provided in every room in case you can't wait to try the bottle that you picked up earlier. There is plenty of extra seating in each room for enjoying the wine and other treats found on your journeys. None of the rooms have air conditioning, but all are equipped with floor fans. Even after a hot day, the temperature will significantly drop in the evening, making sleeping pleasant; this area of Michigan rarely suffers from extremes in temperatures.

The large common area offers several individual spaces for conversation or relaxation. A large fireplace is surrounded by leather furnishings, giving the comfortable niche an outdoorsy look. The screened porch has a tile floor and wicker furniture, and also functions as the information center for the area, with plenty of brochures available for your perusal.

The dining room showcases Sandy's apple collection. She collects Wall pottery, which is displayed throughout the room. We enjoyed a scrumptious and filling multi-course breakfast and great conversation at the table with the Lambdins and the other guests. For lunch you might try the restaurant in Suttons Bay that Sandy's son operates. He will also cater special meals at the Manitou Manor; Sandy can provide details on both options. A great spot for dinner is the Leelanau Country Inn, on M-22, just a few miles from the inn. It has been ranked as the best place to eat on the peninsula.

Opportunities abound for all sorts of recreational activities in the area: dune climbing, hiking, canoeing, skiing, boating, or just relaxing. Be sure to take your bathing suit along on your bike ride as there are beaches along both routes. Of course, there is always the time-worn tradition of petoskey hunting on the Lake Michigan beaches. The petoskey, a fossilized colony coral, is found along the shoreline between the cities of Petoskey and Traverse City. Its unusual appearance makes it an intriguing specimen. You'll find some in the garden at the Manitou Manor; your hosts will gladly offer suggestions as to which beaches to comb for these treasures.

This region is world renowned for its cherry orchards and related products. Guests can pick their own cherries at the orchard just outside of the inn. Throughout the peninsula, you'll find market stands with tasty treats, fresh off the trees. Wine production also thrives on the peninsula because of the temperate climate. In fact, this part of Michigan shares the same latitude as some of the great vineyards in France. An amazing variety of wines are produced here, and most wineries have tasting rooms and retail outlets. To promote the local fruit, many even bottle a cherry wine.

Biking from Manitou Manor

Terrain: The roads along the coast are flat to rolling. The interior becomes very hilly, for those seeking a good workout.

Road Conditions: The road surfaces are good, and there is a wide shoulder approaching Glen Arbor.

Traffic: Usually light, traffic often increases on weekends and holidays because this, after all, is a resort area.

Mountain Biking Opportunities: Leelanau Trail; for details, inquire at the Northport Pedaler.

Nearest Bike Shop
Northport Pedaler
115 E. Nagonaba
Northport, MI 49670
Phone: (213) 386-5644

Manitou Manor to Glen Arbor (out and back, 32.2 miles)
This route provides views of Lake Michigan and Little Traverse Lake. Along the way, you'll pass through the Sleeping Bear Dunes National Lakeshore. In Glen Arbor, you will find easy access to Lake Michigan by turning right on most of the roads in town. There are good restaurants here, as well as touristy shops.

Cume	Turn	Street/Landmark
0.0	R	**M-22**
4.8	R	**E. Traverse**
7.6	R	**M-22**
15.0	TA	Junction with **M-109** (Glen Arbor)
32.2	L	Manitou Manor

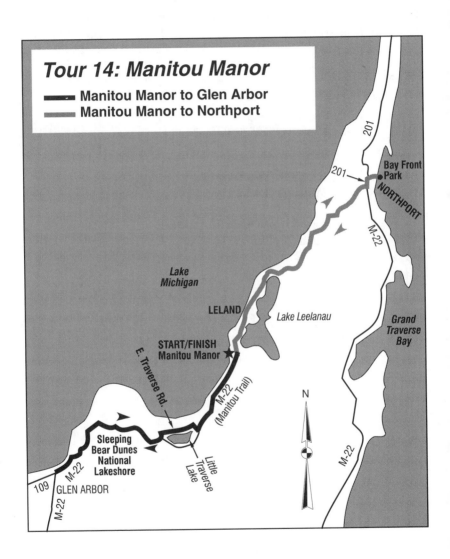

Tour 14: Manitou Manor

■■■ Manitou Manor to Glen Arbor
▬▬ Manitou Manor to Northport

201

Bay Front
•Park

201

NORTHPORT

M-22

Lake
Michigan

LELAND

Lake Leelanau

Grand
Traverse
Bay

START/FINISH
Manitou Manor ★

E. Traverse Rd.

M-22
(Manitou Trail)

N

M-22

Sleeping
Bear Dunes
National
Lakeshore

Little
Traverse
Lake

109
GLEN ARBOR
M-22

Manitou Manor to Northport (out and back, 29.6 miles)

This route passes through Leland, a low-key town with several restaurants and shops. Follow the sign to the ferry to visit Fishtown to experience an old market town. From some of the hills on this route you will get an excellent view of the lake. Northport is at the tip of the Peninsula; if you have the time and energy, you might enjoy a ride to the lighthouse at the state park. Northport also has all services and a nice beachfront park, which is the turn-around point on this ride.

Cume	Turn	Street/Landmark
0.0	L	**M-22**
3.0	-	Town of Leland
14.3	L	**Rt. 201 (Westbay Rd.)**
14.5	R	**Main** (Follow 201)
14.6	S	To lake
14.8	TA	**Bay Front Park** (Northport)
15.1	L	**Main** (Follow 201)
15.3	R	**M-22**
29.6	R	Manitou Manor

The Munro House

202 Maumee Street
Jonesville, MI 49250
Phone: (517) 849-9292; (800) 320-3792
Web: www.getaway2smi.com/munro
Innkeepers: Mike and Laurie Venturini
Rates: Budget to Deluxe

"The capacity for delight is the gift of paying attention."
— Julia Cameron

An imposing Greek Revival mansion, The Munro House, circa 1834, was the first brick house in the county and required several years to complete. The interior is more opulent than the exterior, but not pretentious; "Elegant, but comfy," is the description favored by the innkeepers. The sumptuous parlors reminded us of the lobby of an elegant hotel or men's club.

The first resident of the house was George C. Munro, a brigadier general in the Civil War. His family and descendants occupied the house for nearly a century. Once a station on the Underground Railroad, the house contains a secret room; the innkeepers will be glad to show it to you if there are no guests staying in the adjoining room.

This gracious home flaunts a variety of architectural features. Note the built-in window shutters, based on a design of Thomas Jefferson. The high ceilings, decorative woodwork, and chandeliers invite closer inspection and admiration. Ten fireplaces—some in the guestrooms and others in the public areas—entice guests to enjoy the warmth of the fire and provide a focal point for gatherings. The spacious main sitting area, as well as the smaller and cozier reading room, invite guests to get comfortable in these plush surroundings, with diversions such as games, books, and video tapes.

Beyond the living area, the long table in the dining room is the perfect place to enjoy a take-out pizza or to spread out route maps. You'll be tempted to linger and enjoy the variety of cookies that are baked fresh daily.

At the very back of the house, the colonial-style kitchen, with a large hearth and several cloth-covered tables, is where guests gather to enjoy a made-to-order breakfast—an uncommon feature, especially for an inn this size. We enjoyed pancakes produced by the Kerry Company, a local mill. Breakfast hours are flexible to suit the schedules of the mix of corporate and casual guests.

What is really impressive about the Munro House is the various styles of décor throughout. While many establishments stick with variations of a common theme, the seven rooms at the Munro House include rustic, romantic, Shaker, and garden. No two rooms resemble each other even remotely. Since some rooms were occupied, we only got to glimpse a few; however from those we did see, it can be assumed that all meet the same high standards found throughout the inn.

Six of the seven rooms occupy the second story of the house, reached by a massive and ornate staircase. Clara's Room has its own private staircase at the rear of the house, and is perfect for those seeking solitude. A hand-painted tree on the wall adds drama to this bright and airy room, which is guaranteed to energize its occupants. For relaxation, the Jacuzzi tub aims to please muscle-fatigued cyclists.

Adjacent to this room, The George Room fittingly replicates an outdoorsy, rustic style reminiscent of the first settlers who arrived in this rugged territory. The bed has pine posts, and a moose head dominates the wall. Fishing scenes complete the picture. Those early settlers might have enjoyed the whirlpool tub that sits in a corner of this spacious room.

When you step down into The Shaker room, you'll find two queen-size beds and a simple and traditional décor. A peg rail around the perimeter and plank floors throughout give the room an air of authenticity. Quilts cover the beds, and a fireplace with a Grandma Moses-style painting above it will warm you on those chilly nights. Shaker boxes on the floor and a braided rug maintain the simple scheme of this room beneath the eaves.

The Maumee Room appeals to the garden lover. Floral wallpaper accented by shades of green, white, and pink give this light and feminine room the atmosphere of a greenhouse. The fourposter bed shines under its lace canopy and bow-tied posts. The total effect creates a relaxing and comfortable retreat.

The Sauk Trail Room has old maps, a musket, and looks much like the officers' rooms exhibited in the museums at Gettysburg or Vicksburg. The camp-style bed and large wood-planked floor remind one of an encampment. A wood-burning fireplace suits this room well. Staying in this room may give you the sense that you traveled through these parts by Conestoga wagon.

Our room, The Garden Room, had a very interesting old wallpaper motif. The paper on the ceiling encroached on the wall space, creating a very interesting border effect. Candle sconces on the wall contributed to the old-fashioned, yet elegant look of the room. Because the private bathroom is small, an antique dresser has been modified into a vanity that fits perfectly among the room's other furnishings. A white mantel surrounds the fireplace, situated next to the queen-size brass bed.

All of the rooms have air conditioning, an armoire to disguise the television, and private baths. A closet in the hallway contains extras that guests may have forgotten, including a pair of pajamas. Whatever you need, you'll find it here.

There are several notable attractions in this region. The Grosvenor House, designed by the same architect who planned the state Capitol, is listed on the National Register of Historic Places and is open to the public. Hillsdale College has an attractive campus that you'll see as you pass through it on one of the rides below. While there are some hills, the terrain is more rolling and the scenery is very easy on the eyes. The town of Allen is a renowned antiques center, but it seemed a disappointment after all the hype we had heard about it. Litchfield, the destination for the other ride, is a very peaceful town. If you are lucky, you might see an Amish buggy along the roadside. The Munro House is also located near the Sauk Trail, a well-known Indian trading route that ran from the Mississippi to Detroit. You will notice a portrait of Chief Baw Breese, a Potawotami leader and local tribesman, hanging in the dining room.

Biking from The Munro House

Terrain: The roads gently undulate.

Road Conditions: Roads are all paved and in good condition. There are shoulders along the busier roads.

Traffic: Light to moderate in the town of Hillsdale.

Nearest Bike Shop
Kickstand Schwinn Cyclery
41 West Chicago Street
Coldwater, MI 49036-1616
Phone: (517) 279-6208

Munro House to Litchfield (28.1 miles)
Litchfield is a charming town just north of Jonesville. Watch for Amish horses and buggies making rounds throughout the area. Allen is renowned for its antiques. The route also passes through some lovely wooded areas. Take care while riding through Hillsdale, as traffic can get heavy.

Cume	Turn	Street/Landmark
0.0	**L**	**Maumee**
0.1	**S**	Cross US 12, name changes to **Evans** and then **Homer**
7.3	-	Town of Litchfield; small park at intersection of 99 and 49
7.3	**L/L**	**W. St. Joe**, followed by a quick left onto **Chicago Street (M-49)**

Cume	Turn	Street/Landmark
10.4	R	**Genessee**
10.9	L	**Allen**
13.9	L	**US 12**; town of Allen
14.5	R	**M-49 (Eden Rd.)**
17.0	L	**Bacon**
19.0	R	**Sand Lake**
19.2	L	**Bacon**
22.1	L	**Spring**
23.0	L	**Lewis**
23.2	L	**M-99** (Watch for **Bike Route** on right side shortly after turning)
27.6	R	**Chicago (US 12)**
28.0	R	**Maumee**
28.1		Munro House

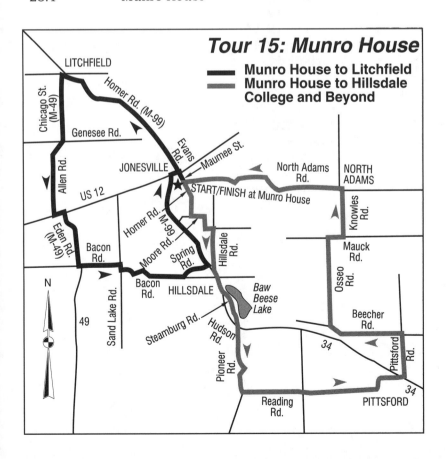

Tour 15: Munro House

▬▬ **Munro House to Litchfield**
▬▬ **Munro House to Hillsdale College and Beyond**

Munro House to Hillsdale College and beyond (37.6 miles)

The Hillsdale College campus, with its beautiful fraternity houses and buildings, is a pleasant place to tour. Beyond the campus, you will reach a woodland area and pass through shady forests with lake views. The roads are rolling, and the busier roads have good shoulders.

Cume	Turn	Street/Landmark
0.0	R	**Maumee**
1.4	S	**Homer** (main road bears left)
2.0	L	**Moore**
3.4	R	**Hillsdale**
5.3	BL	Name changes to **Broad (M-99)**; Hillsdale Town Center
6.2	L	**Steamburg** (lake view)
8.1	L	**Hudson (M-99)**
11.0	R	**Pioneer (M-99)**; gas station
13.6	L	**Reading** (follow curves and stay on paved road)
18.3	L	**Pittsford**
18.8	-	Town of Pittsford (convenience store, gas station)
20.4	L	**Beecher**
23.5	R	**Osseo**
27.5	R	**Mauk** (follow paved road)
28.0	L	**Knowles**
30.0	L	**W. Main**, becomes **N. Adams** outside of town
37.2	R	**Maumee**
37.6		Munro House

White Swan Inn

303 Mears Avenue
Whitehall, MI 49461
Phone: 888-WHT SWAN
E-mail: whtswan@mc.cns.net
Web: www.bbonline.com/mi/whiteswan
Innkeepers: Cathy and Ron Russell
Rates: Budget

Probably the first visitor to the first family in Whitehall first asked the question, "But what do you do with yourselves here all year?" Practically every visitor since has repeated the question. And practically every resident has felt a vague wonderment that such a question would ever enter anybody's mind.

From *100 Years Whitehall Michigan 1860-1960* by Louis J. Berman

Thanks to its prime location near the Lake Michigan Shoreline, Whitehall and the surrounding area bursts with activity. These days, visitors to Whitehall who don't know what to do with themselves simply aren't trying very hard. Lighthouses, state parks, cottages, and roadside picnic areas attract visitors in throngs. Closer to town, White Lake provides a plethora of on- and off-water activities. The village has spiffed itself up to be presentable to tourists, with streets lined with well-maintained homes and trendy shops in the business area.

Although we aren't related, innkeepers Cathy and Ron Russell and I have a few things in common besides the same last name. Cathy and I come from the same town, and even attended the same high school at the same time. We didn't know each other then, but before we left the White Swan Inn it certainly seemed that we were old lost friends. Cathy had lived in a historic district in Toledo where many of the homes had two sets of staircases. She envied those with the double sets of stairs and hoped one day to have a home with this special amenity. She found it in Whitehall, Michigan.

The White Swan Inn is a traditional Victorian with a wrap-around porch where guests can sit and watch the passersby or enjoy a view of the garden. With white wicker tables and chairs, the screened-in porch lends itself to reading, sipping a glass of iced tea, or visiting with other guests. Inside, the grand living room is tastefully enlivened with shades of green, rose, and white. The light brown wicker furniture, antique liquor cabinet, and green uphol-stered chair make a smooth transition from the porch. The large bay windows have shutters topped with a lace valance, and the frames on the pocket doors are finished with impressive fretwork.

Cathy uses bold colors throughout the inn, to pleasant effect. The dining room is a melange of greens and golds. Upholstered chairs surround the dining table, and a chandelier hangs from above. In this room, Cathy serves a delectable breakfast of home-baked specialties. Once the aroma of breakfast wafts through the inn, late-rising guests practically leap from their beds.

Sleeping quarters are on the second floor. The Cygnet Room is the largest of these, furnished with a king-size bed with an oak and wicker headboard; it can be transformed into two twins, if necessary. The natural wood floor matches the intensity of the wood on the window shutters. Green, blue, pink, and white hues are used throughout the room to lighten the effect of the wood. A private bath is located down the hall, and right next door is a small lounge area were guests are welcome to fix a beverage, grab a homemade snack, or simply relax.

The Covell Room, named in honor of the first owners, is a very elegant retreat. The deep colors—green, burgundy, and gold—lend the room a royal air, which you can enjoy from the wicker rocking chair. The green carpet under your feet is a lush cushion to sink your toes into. The adjacent bath has a deep step-down tub for soaking and soothing your muscles after a ride, and a hand-held shower to make washing your hair a simple chore. There is also a third, smaller guestroom with a private bath that was occupied at the time of our visit.

Cathy has energy to spare, and uses one of the rooms in her house as a shop selling many locally-produced items. It's always impossible to resist homemade hot fudge. Other products include stationery, t-shirts with the White Swan logo imprinted on them, and other items like handmade soap and sachets. She plans to move this wee little shop to the carriage house in the back that she hopes to convert soon.

Biking from The White Swan Inn

Montague, a neighboring town of Whitehall, is the terminus for the Hart-Montague rail-trail, one of the first in the state and a model for other rails-to-trails projects. It passes through woodlands and a few small towns, gradually climbing to the other terminus in Hart, 25 miles away. The trail is an attraction in itself, and the tourist bureau has a nice booklet that lists other attractions and services along the trail.

One of these services is the Mexican restaurant in Hart. Always being on a tight schedule, we embarked on our journey rather late in the day, not thinking that it takes time to order and get served in a restaurant. We reached the restaurant uneventfully and had a relaxing meal—only to realize toward the end of a filling and delicious dinner that we still had to ride back a long way and didn't have lights. Dusk lingered for awhile and we thought that we could still make it, but darkness soon dropped like a heavy curtain. Fortunately, we could see the clearing in the woods and somehow stayed on the path.

We felt confident that we would make it back to the inn, but were startled when something crossed our path. How fortuitous for the herd of deer crossing the trail in front of us—and how lucky for us—that we didn't collide. Fearing another more intimate encounter, our hearts beat faster as we cautiously looked left and right trying to discern any shadows or movements in the darkness. Eventually, we saw a faint light in the distance, signaling that we were approaching the trail head. The ride on the city streets—sans bike lights—took us past a police car. Fortunately for us, we either couldn't be seen at all or the officer simply ignored us. Our innkeepers, concerned about our well-being, were considering sending out a search party. We apologized for causing them to worry and stressed that our behavior was neither safe nor typical. So, a word to the wise: Before you venture out to an irresistible destination, be sure that you have the appropriate gear with you to complete your ride in safety.

Terrain: Reasonably flat.

Road Conditions: Good.

Traffic: Light.

Nearest Bike Shop
Breakaway Bicycles
2145 West Sherman Boulevard
Muskegon, MI 49441-3434
Phone: (616) 759-0001

The Hart-Montague Trail (up to 48.6 miles)
Once you get on the trail, you will have the option of biking out as far as you wish. The trail rises slightly on the way to Hart. There are small towns along the way, and an excellent reference for services in these towns along the trail is a booklet called _Hart-Montague Bicycle Trail State Park Guide,_ by JB Publications. Check for a copy at the tourism office. You will need to buy a permit for the trail, which may be purchased at the carry-out store next to the trailhead. A daily family pass costs $5 and individual pass is $2. There are plans to extend the trail at the southern end (Montague).

Directions from the inn to the trailhead:

Cume	Turn	Street/Landmark
0.0	**R**	**Mears**
0.2	**L**	**Colby** (at traffic light)
0.8	**R**	**Water** (at traffic light)
1.3		**Trailhead** on right; get pass at the store on the left
-		The trail continues for 23 miles to the town of Hart

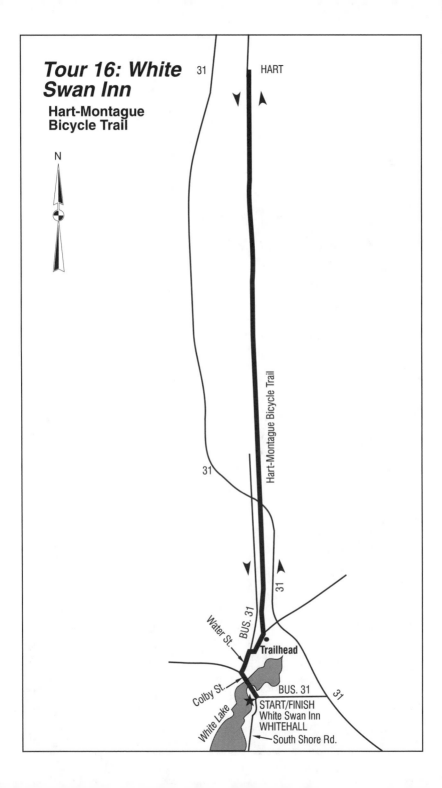

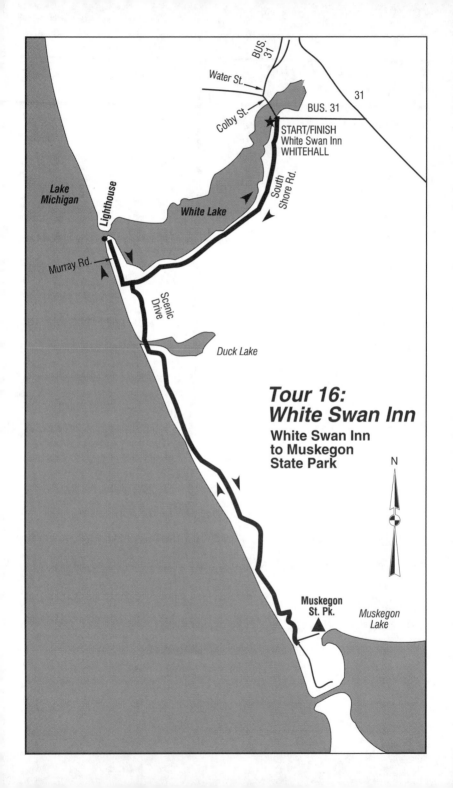

BUS. 31

Water St.

Colby St.

31

BUS. 31

START/FINISH
White Swan Inn
WHITEHALL

Lake
Michigan

Lighthouse

White Lake

South Shore Rd.

Murray Rd.

Scenic
Drive

Duck Lake

Tour 16:
White Swan Inn

White Swan Inn
to Muskegon
State Park

N

Muskegon
St. Pk.

Muskegon
Lake

Directions from the Montague trailhead back to the inn:

Cume	Turn	Street/Landmark
0.0	L	**Water**
0.5	L	**Colby** (at traffic light)
1.1	R	**Mears**
1.3	L	White Swan

White Swan to Muskegon State Park (31.1 miles)
This refreshing ride near the Lake Michigan coast offers great lake views, beaches, marinas, a lighthouse, and a hiking trail along the shoreline. Be sure to bring your swimsuit. There is a nice visitor's center at the lighthouse, and Muskegon State Park is a great place for a picnic.

0.0	L	**Slocum**
0.1	L	**S. Lake**
2.0	-	**Lake** becomes **South Shore**
3.3	R	**South Shore**
5.4	S	Through intersection, becomes **Murray Rd.**
6.7	L	To lighthouse
6.8	-	Lighthouse
6.9	R	**Murray**
8.3	R	**Scenic Drive**
8.6	R	**Scenic Drive**
16.3	-	Ruth Ann's Ice Cream
16.5	TA	Muskegon State Park entrance; turn around here and go left on **Scenic Dr.**
24.4	L	**Scenic Drive**
24.7	R	**South Shore**
27.8	L	**South Shore**
29.1	-	**South Shore** becomes **S. Lake**
31.0	R	**Slocum**
31.1		White Swan Inn

Will O'Glenn Irish Bed & Breakfast, Glenn, Michigan

Will O'Glenn Irish Bed and Breakfast

1286 64ᵗʰ Street
P.O. Box 288
Glenn, MI 49416
Phone: (888) 237-3009
Fax: (616) 227-3045
E-mail: shamrock@irish-inn.com
Web: www.irish-inn.com/
Innkeepers: Ward and Shelley Gahan
Rates: Moderate to Deluxe

May the road rise to meet you. May the wind be always at your back. May the sun shine warm upon you face, the rains fall soft upon your fields and, until we meet again, may God hold you in the palm of his hand. — Irish proverb

Ward Gahan, a native of County Tipperary, Ireland, exhibits pride in his heritage throughout the Will O'Glenn Bed and Breakfast. There are reminders of his homeland everywhere you turn. Even before you enter the inn, you'll probably be greeted by his massive dog, Madra—an Irish wolfhound, naturally. Here in the middle of nowhere, in a setting that offers peace, quiet, and excellent stargazing, you could easily forget that you are near Lake Michigan rather than the Irish Sea.

The inn, originally a combination antique shop, classic car museum, and home, has been retrofitted to emulate an Irish homestead. Upon entering the inn, you will notice a large common room to the left, complete with a wood-burning stove (alas, peat isn't easy to come by in these parts) for those chilly days. Several comfortable couches and chairs are arranged throughout the room. If that doesn't warm you up, you can sidle up to the bar and warm yourself with a refreshment (you supply the spirits). Retrieved by the previous owners from a Moose lodge, this cozy bar area replicates an Irish pub. If you prefer a more formal setting for relaxing or mingling with other guests, you'll find another room, removed from the great room, with an outstanding view of the beautiful surroundings.

Next to the bar is the kitchen, where breakfast is prepared. Guests are welcome to use the kitchen and help themselves to tea, coffee, and cold beverages there. When Shelley prepares the traditional Irish breakfast, be prepared for a feast: white and black pudding, rashers, eggs, Irish bread, and that wonderful Barry's Irish tea. For those on a cholesterol-restricted diet, be sure to let Shelley know beforehand, as these treats will surely raise your level. Fortunately, cycling will burn off some of those calories, so be adventurous.

Breakfast is served in the large and pleasant dining room. Shelley will tell you the process for making the perfect cup of tea. I was surprised that her instructions were exactly the way we prepare tea at home.

Four differently decorated bedrooms provide accommodations for inn guests. All have private baths, Irish literature, and a surprising touch—Irish colognes, for a real sense of Ireland.

On the first floor, The Tipperary Hunt Room pays homage to an Irish tradition. The décor is reminiscent of a lodge style, with green, brown, burgundy, and beige comprising the color scheme. Hunting pictures and throws accessorize the spacious room, which also boasts a fireplace. The hunting theme is carried through to the private bathroom. For a good soak after a day of riding, you'll find a whirlpool nestled in an alcove.

The Emerald Room, like the remaining guestrooms, is located on the second floor. The Gahans have refrained from using "a thousand shades of green"—a phrase often used to describe verdant Ireland—but have accented the green with barn red, clay, yellow, and gold. The total effect is enchanting. A floral canopy covers the queen-size bed, and a fireplace provides warmth and atmosphere. Separating the Emerald Room from the other rooms is a small common area, which contains sofas, a TV, and of course, Irish magazines.

The spacious Claddagh Room, named after the ring that symbolizes love, friendship, and loyalty, contains two double beds. It is the perfect place for friends who are sharing a room but need to spread out. A maple tree out front casts a cooling shade into the room.

Translated into English, the name of the Tir na n'Og Room promises to bring eternal youth to the occupants. You can read up on the legend from the book in the room, while enjoying the carefree moments of youth. There is a king-size bed, and a deck overlooking the herb garden.

The grounds themselves are lovely, and an enchanting summerhouse in the back is the perfect spot to read or relax and enjoy the bird songs. From the solitude of this retreat, you may catch a glimpse of deer, pheasants, or other wildlife. You are welcome to explore the grounds; Ward has cut paths for your walking pleasure. Several garden areas add color and scent to the premises.

If all the offerings at the inn aren't enough to keep you occupied and leave you any free time, you'll find plenty of diversions in the area in addition to cycling. This region is renowned for its fruit—especially blueberries. Pick your own, or visit one of the many pre-picked fruit stands. You'll even find a winery nearby. Antiques, harbor towns, and sandy beaches offer ample opportunity to pass the time away.

South Haven, a picturesque harborside town, lures visitors to enjoy its waterfront location, view exquisite old homes, or sample the shops along its pleasant streets. If you find the time, you might enjoy exploring the Kal-Haven State Park, a linear state park that continues over 30 miles to just outside of Kalamazoo. Perfect for cycling, hiking, or cross-country skiing, this trail traverses diverse terrain.

In the other direction, trendy Saugatuck contrasts with South Haven. Reminiscent of a small New England town, the tree-lined streets shade visitors from the summer sun. Unusual items can be found in the eclectic mix of shops, and a wide variety of gastronomic delights garnish the menus of the local restaurants. The chain ferry runs frequently and is a unique experience that shouldn't be missed.

Back at the inn, Ward and Shelly offer a medley of theme-based events. If you catch Ward, you may even get a chance to learn some traditional Irish dancing. Whether you choose to partake of the arranged events or explore on your own, your stay at the Will O'Glenn will be fulfilling.

Biking from Will O'Glenn

Terrain: Being fairly close to the coast, the roads are relatively flat with some slightly rolling sections.

Road Conditions: The condition of the roads is good.

Traffic: As you approach the towns of Saugatuck and South Haven, you will notice an increase in congestion, but in general the routes carry little traffic.

Mountain Biking Opportunities: The Kal-Haven Trail starts just outside of South Haven. It is 30+ miles of hard-packed gravel, and not technically difficult.

Nearest Bike Shop
Outpost Sports
114 Dykman
South Haven, MI 49090
Phone: (616) 637-5555

Will O'Glenn to South Haven (26.8 miles)
This route passes blueberry farms, cornfields on undulating roads, and some shady areas. A few of the roads are hard-packed gravel. South Haven is a delightful harbor town with a nearby beach.

Cume	Turn	Street/Landmark
0.0	R	64th
1.0	R	111th
3.0	L	68th
5.1	R	107th
6.6	L	71st
9.0	R	103rd

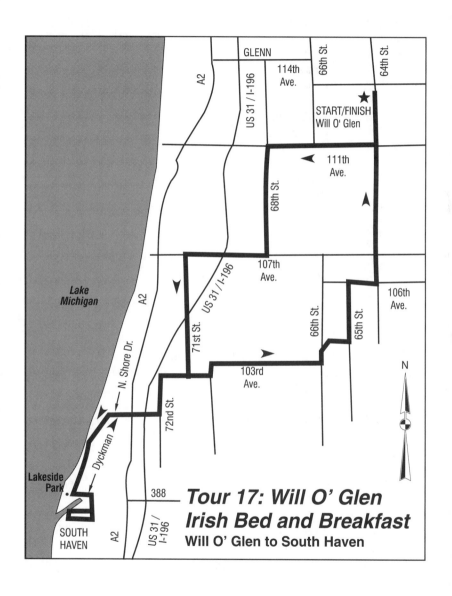

GLENN

66th St.

64th St.

A2

114th
Ave.

US 31 / I-196

★
START/FINISH
Will O' Glen

◄ 111th
Ave.

68th St.

▲

Lake
Michigan

A2

▼

US 31 / I-196

107th
Ave.

106th
Ave.

71st St.

66th St.

65th St.

N. Shore Dr.

►

103rd
Ave.

72nd St.

N

Dyckman

Lakeside
Park

388

SOUTH
HAVEN

A2

US 31 /
I-196

*Tour 17: Will O' Glen
Irish Bed and Breakfast*
Will O' Glen to South Haven

Cume	Turn	Street/Landmark
9.5	L	**72nd**
10.2	R	**N. Shore**
12.7	-	**Lakeside Park**—facilities
12.8	L	**Dyckman**
13.2	R	**Broadway**
13.4	R	**Phoenix** (downtown South Haven)
13.6	R	**Center**
13.7	R	**Williams**
13.9	L	**Dyckman**
14.2	R	**N. Shore**
16.7	L	**72nd**
17.5	R	**103rd**
18.5	L	**70th**
18.7	R	**103rd**
20.8	L	**66th**
21.0	R	**103rd**
21.6	L	**65th**
22.7	R	**106th** (gravel)
23.2	L	**64th**
26.8		Will O'Glenn

Will O'Glenn to Saugatuck (32.7 miles)

Get an early start to have time to enjoy the many stops along this route. Douglas has its own charms and is worth exploring. The Fenn Valley winery offers tastings; just remember that you still have to ride about 6 more miles after this stop. Besides the small towns along the way, you'll pass orchards, berry farms, and artists studios.

Cume	Turn	Street/Landmark
0.0	L	**64th**
0.1	L	**113th**
1.1	R	**66th**
1.6	L	**114th**
3.6	R	**70th** (town of Glenn)
3.9	BL	**70th** becomes **Lakeshore**
7.4	-	Westside County Park

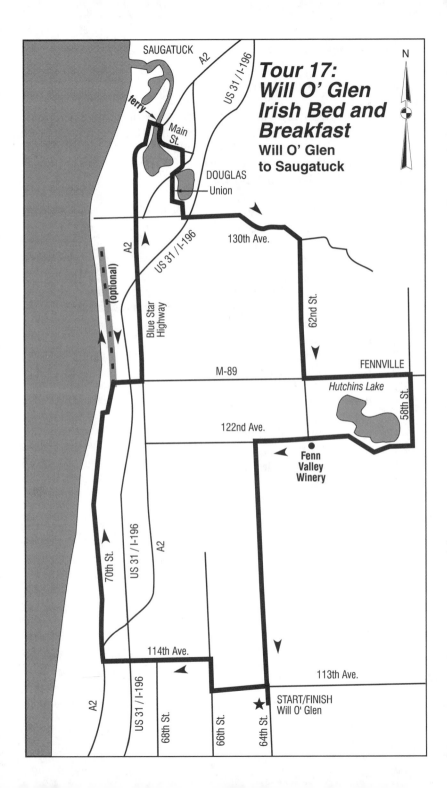

Cume	Turn	Street/Landmark
8.9	R	**M-89** (*Note: Side trip for Lake Michigan view:* continue straight along Lakeshore for 2.1 miles instead of turning right on M-89. Turn around at the "Dead End" sign, ride 2.1 miles back, and turn left on M-89 to continue route.
9.3	L	**Blue Star Highway**
12.4	L	**Ferry St.**
14.0	-	**Chain Ferry**—board this to continue route—the ferry runs continuously. When you reach the other side, pick up cues below.
14.0	R	**Water St.**
14.3	-	Bike rack, information booth, park (Saugatuck)
14.9	R	**Blue Star Highway** (if you aren't comfortable on the highway, you can use the sidewalk)
15.2	L	**Main**
15.6	R	**South** (town of Douglas)
15.7	L	**Union**
15.9	BL	Stay on **Union**
16.2	L	**Wiley** (becomes 130th and then Riverside)
18.9	R	**62nd**
21.6	L	**M-89**
23.6	R	**58th** (town of Fennville)
24.9	R	**122nd**
26.6	-	Fenn Valley Winery
28.0	L	**64th**
32.7		Will O'Glenn

Ohio

"There is little about Ohio that is surprising. On the other hand there is much that is interesting and a great deal that is unknown or little appreciated." — Roderick Peattie, *Geography of Ohio*, 1923

As Peattie suggests above, you will find much that is interesting as you tour through Ohio on your bicycle: a national park just outside of Cleveland, a beautiful valley that reminded author Louis Bromfield so much of France that he settled there, and the rolling Amish country of eastern Ohio.

A wide variety of terrain from the flat Lake Plains in the north to the glaciated hills of the south offer unique opportunities for all levels of cyclists. For those who enjoy a bit of both types of terrain, there are even some areas where one direction will offer a quite challenging ride, while the other will seem mild in comparison.

Ohio claims the largest Amish community in the world, canal towns, the Cuyahoga Valley Recreation Area and numerous rail trails. Historic towns like Marietta and Grand Rapids hold their own special charms, with Marietta showcasing its river town attractions while Grand Rapids focuses on its canal town identity. Chillicothe offers a look into the past as well as many outdoor opportunities right outside of the city limits.

Castles and caves just beyond West Liberty attract many visitors. The Cuyahoga Valley provides a plethora of activities and attractions within its boundaries. Good home cooking, great scenery, and a unique culture are the draws of the Amish country in New Bedford. The Lake Erie Islands, Lakeshore Drive, and Chautagua Institute prove popular on Marblehead Peninsula. The Great Black Swamp area near Archbold entices visitors with Sauder Village and Goll Woods. A proudly promoted feature near Alpha is the Little Miami Rail Trail, stretching north and south through the center of the state. Nestled in a valley surrounded by rolling hills, tiny Lucas revels in the shadows of the nearby hills and forests.

Interesting, yes. Unknown? Possibly. But once you visit the inns in this section, take some of the rides, and visit the local attractions, you'll certainly come away with a great appreciation for Ohio and all it has to offer.

Alpha House

758 Alpha Road
P.O. Box 140
Alpha, OH 45301
Phone: (800) 337-2852
Innkeepers: Jackie and Bob Jackson
Rates: Budget to Moderate

> *May-day in the morning, sunshine in the sky,*
> *See the merry boys and girls wave a gay "good-bye."*
> *Bikes in shining order, luncheon in a kit,*
> *What a happy, wholesome way a loving trail to hit.*
> *Mother in the doorway, looking on with pride,*
> *Little brother wishing he could with them ride.*
> *Flowers and birds and laughter to cheer them on the way,*
> *Say, you can't beat biking, on a morn in May.*
> *—The Saturday Evening Post,* May 18, 1929

How fortuitous for Jackie and Bob Jackson that the H-Connector to the popular Little Miami Trail passes right by Alpha House. The Jacksons enjoy watching the people go by while sitting in the common room of their inn or fixing breakfast. Jackie doesn't hesitate to comment that she welcomes cyclists with open arms, and says that they are among her best guests.

Anybody would love Alpha House. A spacious old building that has served as a general store, post office, and apartments, it has been transformed into a very comfortable B&B. Downstairs you'll find many accents with a bicycling theme: old magazine ads, planters, a solar-powered cyclist, and other curiosities. Even their brochure shares the bicycling theme. As a bonus, the Jacksons allow guests to borrow their bikes—a gesture especially appreciated by those guests who were unaware of the proximity of the trail.

What first impresses the guests upon entering the Alpha House is the homey feeling that permeates the home. Cozy areas for relaxing or curling up with a book are scattered throughout the lower level. Jackie leaves snacks and beverages in the kitchen and guests are welcome to help themselves. Although they live off the premises, the Jacksons return bright and early every morning to prepare a sumptuous breakfast that is served at the country dining table. Our breakfast included Belgian waffles, a sausage casserole, fruit, coffee cake, tea and coffee and juice. The morning of our visit, we were fortunate to enjoy the company of Ed Dressler and his wife. Ed is affiliated with the rail trail project.

Upstairs are 3 bedrooms, one with a private bath and two that share another bath. At the top of the stairs you'll find the Country Room, the name of which appropriately describes the style of the furnishings and décor of this casual room. One nice accessory in this room is a tape player, with a selection of tapes from which to choose. A television is also included should you have the time for additional entertainment. A ledge around the perimeter of the room is claimed by a variety of stuffed animals, and there is a private bath.

The Victorian Room, where we stayed, has the décor to match its name. A nice armoire holding a TV, a lovely reproduction bed, and a small table with chairs fill this very cozy room. Along the ledges are simple accoutrements that complement the décor. During our visit, the room also featured a strange bleating sound. A search for the source of the recurring noise led us to the closet, where we found a curious toy lamb.

Further down the hall, the Shaker Room has two queen-sized Shaker-style beds with quilts made by Jackie; in fact, Jackie made all the quilts throughout the inn. A plank floor adds authenticity to the Shaker theme of this room, which is brightened by several windows. Tables and chairs are also provided for seating convenience.

For those sharing the bathroom, there is a vanity in the hallway outside the bathroom as well as a full bathroom. This arrangement eliminates the possibility of having to wait to brush your teeth or wash your hands. Sponges and squeegies are provided for cleaning up after yourself—a thoughtful and practical accessory that every shared bath should have. Indeed, Jackie has thought of everything. One very nice rule she abides by is that *all* the linens—including the top covers of the bed—are laundered after each guest's stay. For those of us who wonder who has breathed on the covers, this is a much-appreciated gesture.

The Jacksons will gladly suggest some cycling destinations along the trail, as well as other activities in the area. One popular seasonal activity is the outdoor drama, *Blue Jacket*. The performance tells the story of the Indian leader Blue Jacket and other local characters, such as Sam Kenton. The drama takes place on the very land where many of the historic events being portrayed took place many years ago.

Another wonderful place to spend some time is the U.S. Air Force Museum, on the Wright Patterson Air Force Base. The museum chronicles the history of aviation and contains 150 aircraft within its hangars.

Biking from The Alpha House
Alpha House occupies a prime location adjacent to the bike path, and this particular bike path—the Creekside Trail—leads to Xenia, which is the hub of several bike paths.

Xenia was the setting of the Sherwood Anderson's novel *Winesburg, Ohio*. The city opened the hub recently, and eventually five different paths will depart from this point. Also on site is a beautifully renovated depot that includes restrooms, water, and various displays. On our visit, we had some difficulty continuing on the trail once we reached this point. Future plans include directional signs at the hub. In the meantime, there are brochures at the depot to keep you apprised of the routes and their distances. Work progresses continually on the development of the trails, which means more options and greater lengths.

The Little Miami Trail, stretching 72 miles from Springfield to Milford, is one of the rail trails that can be accessed from the Xenia hub. The trail is paved and well maintained, and is continually being expanded. You'll find that the further you get from town the fewer users you will encounter. On weekends and holidays, the trail gets inundated with users. Inline skates, cycles, pedestrians, and wheelchairs use this popular path, so be sure to plan accordingly and share the trail courteously.

With the multitude of trails available, there are many options for you to chose in regards to distances, destinations, and attractions. Rather than give route descriptions for one or two of these out and back rides, it's best to just get yourself to the hub (directions below), choose your destination, and go straight. One of our choices was a ride to the ice cream store in Corwin, which was an out-and-back of 40 miles. You could continue beyond Corwin to reach Waynesboro, noted for its antiques. Another ride to the Jersey Dairy, just outside of Yellow Springs, was an out-and-back of 30 miles. Yellow Springs is a quaint town where you'll find a multitude of resplendent homes, interesting shops and eateries, and Antioch College.

Terrain: Flat, with a gentle rise from Xenia to Yellow Springs.

Road Conditions: The various paved trails are well maintained.

Traffic: These paths can be very crowded on the weekends and cater to cyclists, walkers, and inline skaters.

Mountain Biking Opportunities: Caesar Creek State Park in Waynesboro

Nearest Bike Shop
Xenia Bike Shop
203 South Detroit Street
Xenia, OH 45385
Phone: (937) 372-8303

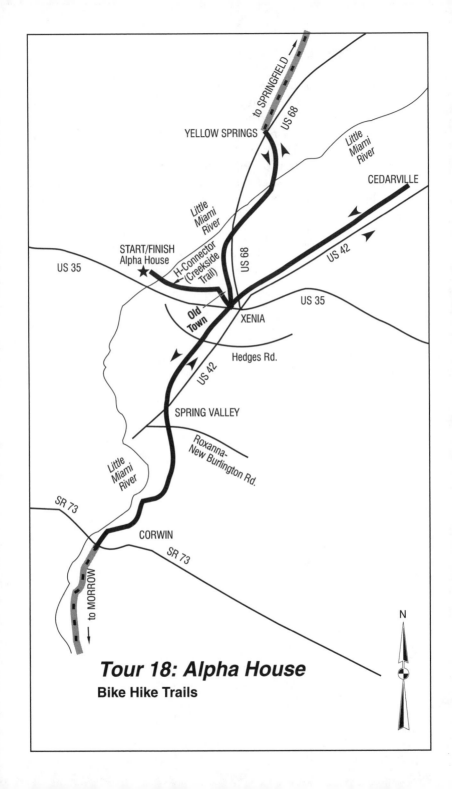

to SPRINGFIELD →

US 68

YELLOW SPRINGS

Little Miami River

CEDARVILLE

START/FINISH
Alpha House

Little Miami River

H-Connector (Creekside Trail)

US 35

US 68

US 42

US 35

Old Town

XENIA

Hedges Rd.

US 42

SPRING VALLEY

Roxanna-New Burlington Rd.

Little Miami River

SR 73

CORWIN

SR 73

to MORROW

N

Tour 18: Alpha House

Bike Hike Trails

From Alpha House to the Hub via the Creekside Trail

Go right on the trail toward Xenia. It is 5.7 miles to the Xenia hub from Alpha House. From there, you can go north to Yellow Springs (10 miles) or Springfield (17 miles). Heading south toward Morrow, it is 14 miles to Corwin, where there is an ice cream stop. A new trail to Cedarville is 9 miles. Remember that these are one-way distances, so double them for your total distance. There are restaurants and shops in the small towns along the way.

AngelWoods Hideaway

1983 Pleasant Valley Road
Lucas, OH 44843
Phone: (888) 882-6949, (419) 892-2929
Innkeepers: John and Vic Cochran
Rates: Moderate

The point I wish to make is this—that during all those thirty years, sometimes in the discomfort of war, sometimes during feelings of depression engendered by Germany, but just as often during the warm, conscious pleasure and satisfaction of France or India or the Spanish Pyrenees, I dreamed constantly of my home country, of my grandfather's farm, of Pleasant Valley ... Toward the end I found myself spending more and more of my sleeping hours in the country where I was born and always what I dreamed of was Ohio and my own country. — Louis Bromfield

Pleasant Valley appropriately describes this wonderful region in the heart of Ohio. Along the back roads, you're likely to encounter some of the Amish folk that have settled in the area. Be sure to visit their bakeries, woodshops, and restaurants for diversions throughout your stay.

Another notable inhabitant of the area was author Louis Bromfield. Besides the many novels that he authored, some with the Pleasant Valley as the setting, he also pioneered new farming techniques, using his own farm as an outdoor laboratory. He hobnobbed with the rich and famous; Lauren Bacall and Humphrey Bogart were married at his Malabar Farm Home. The home is now within the boundaries of Malabar State Park and is open to the public for tours. The park service continues the Bromfield legacy by keeping Malabar a working farm and hosting a number of events throughout the year.

AngelWoods Hideaway sits well off the road against a forested backdrop. The imposing wood and stone structure features an inviting tea house in the front, a perfect place to relax and enjoy the sights and smells of this retreat while sipping your favorite beverage.

Upon entering the house you will be welcomed by the vivacious hostess, Vic. She proudly shows off the spacious inn and encourages you to make yourself at home. The sheer size of the inn makes it a great destination for cycling clubs or other large groups. Vic can arrange luncheons, meetings, showers, or whatever your group desires. In fact, Vic prides herself on the service she provides for guests, and if there is something that she hasn't thought of—which is unlikely—she can arrange it.

A few of the extra touches that Vic provides include a generous Welcome Tea, which could substitute for dinner; concierge services; a pet boarding area; an emergency packet in each room with toiletries, sewing kit, aspirin, and other useful items; and of course, a great breakfast. There are other niceties that you'll just have to wait to discover—we wouldn't want to give all of Vic's delightful touches away!

When you return from a bike ride, you may lounge on the patio, take a dip in the in-ground pool, or soak in the hot tub. Or you may simply retreat to one of the five guestrooms. The largest of these is the Honeymoon Suite, which occupies a large portion of the second floor. Rustic in feel, this room contains a queen fourposter bed, loveseat, Amish rocker, a desk and chair, and a fireplace. A private entrance, private deck, and private bath complete this large and comfortable room.

Also on the second floor, the Sunflower Room offers a bright and cheery atmosphere with sunflower accents and a pale blue background. The country décor includes a carved wooden headboard, a blue-and-white checked valance above the window, an Amish rocker, a white baby christening gown on the wall, and a blue stained glass light on the ceiling. The bath connects to the room, but is shared with the French Quarter room across the hall when both rooms have guests.

The French Quarter Room especially appeals to the purple lovers of the world. The pale purple walls with a cut-out border and eucalyptus wreath accentuate the magenta and pink canopy draped above the bed. A basket on the floor holds green, purple, and white bathroom linens as well as body lotion. A table and chair provide working or letter writing space while the green ambergris queen metal bed offers a comfortable place to sleep. The bathroom, shared with the Sunflower Room, is located just across the hall.

The name of the last room on the second floor gives away its decorating theme: The Teddy Bear Room—with a teddy bear border, of course—is covered with a slate gray striped wallpaper which contrasts nicely with the red carpet and white and red floral curtains. This whimsical room contains a desk and chair, rocker, armoire, and a country-style, wooden-framed queen bed. The private bath continues the teddy bear theme with the cutout animal around the pink and white striped wallpaper.

Another bedroom is located on the first floor, but it was being used by a family member during our visit. We did catch a glimpse of it, and it certainly compares favorably to the other rooms.

Several common areas provide space for privacy. Whether you prefer to watch TV or a movie (there is an extensive video collection available for guests) or just read, relax, or visit with other guests, you'll easily find a suitable space.

The huge kitchen and dining area is dominated by a beautiful Amish oak table, where guests are served a sumptuous breakfast by Vic and her husband John.

Outdoors, you'll find the aforementioned pool, hot tub, and patio, as well as plenty of space to enjoy such activities as volleyball, horseshoes, and croquet. For a relaxing walk, stroll through the 46-acre grounds and enjoy nature. If riding your bike hasn't been enough of a workout, you can stay inside and use the exercise equipment.

Local points of interest include several reservoirs and waterways, which offer opportunities for swimming and canoeing. A host of museums can be found in the Mansfield area. The Ohio State Reformatory, featured in several films including *The Shawshank Redemption*, opens for tours on Sundays for the adventurous curiosity seeker.

Biking from AngelWoods Hideaway

Terrain: Be ready for some climbing, followed by quick descents. While not entirely flat, there are a few roads that cover gentle terrain down in the valley.

Road Conditions: The roads are in good condition throughout, although some of the back roads can be narrow at times. This is not usually a problem, because little traffic passes on them.

Traffic: Most of the roads on the route carry little traffic. Be cautious at the off-angle road crossings.

Mountain Biking Opportunities: Webster's Mountain Sports (see below) can direct you to mountain biking trails in the area.

Nearest Bike Shop
Webster's Mountain Sports
225 Grant Street
Butler, OH 44822
(419) 883-3433

AngelWoods to Lucas (26.2 miles)
Be prepared for some challenging climbs and quick descents. The expansive views from the tops of the hills, however, make the climbs to the summits worth the effort, and there are a few gentle sections along the way. Matching a map with the roads in this area is a real challenge. The Spillway and park are a great place for a picnic.

Cume	Turn	Street/Landmark
0.0	**R**	**Pleasant Valley Rd.**
1.8	**BR**	Stay on **Pleasant Valley Rd.**
2.8		Name changes to **Little Washington**

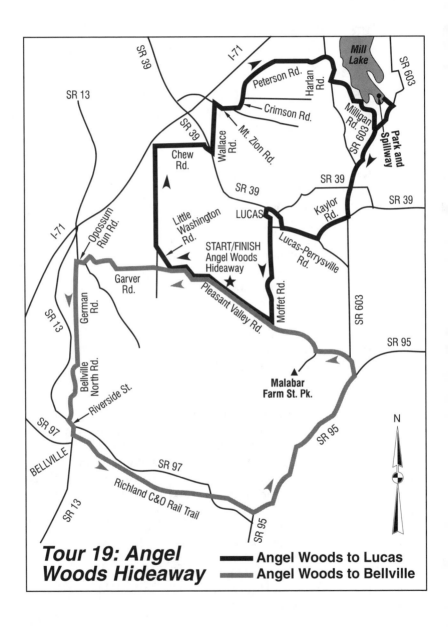

Tour 19: Angel Woods Hideaway

— Angel Woods to Lucas
— Angel Woods to Bellville

Cume	Turn	Street/Landmark
4.8		Name changes to **Chew**
5.0	BR	**Chew**
6.3	BR	**Chew**
6.6	SL	**Chew**
6.7	L	**39**
6.8	BR	**Wallace**, immediately after prior left turn
7.8	-	Fast downhill, *caution*
8.2	R	**Mt. Zion Rd.**
8.6	S	**Crimson** (stop sign)
9.0	S	**Peterson**
10.4	S	At intersection; no sign
11.9	R	**Harlan**
12.6	L	**Milligan**
14.5	L	**SR 603**
15.0	L	Into park and Spillway
15.2	R	**SR 603** (exit park)
18.1	R	**Kaylor**
19.2	R	**Lucas-Perrysville**
20.2	R	Continue on **Lucas-Perrysville** (park, stores, and food in Lucas)
21.9	L	**Moffet** (traffic light)
22.1	BL	After railroad tracks
24.9	R	**Pleasant Valley Rd.**
26.2		AngelWoods

AngelWoods to Belleville (22.6 miles)

The quaint town of Belleville is a nice diversion, and you'll find an ice cream stop in town. Part of the route follows the paved Richland B&O Rail Trail. Louis Bromfield's Malabar Farm is an interesting stop on the way back to the inn, where you can take a guided tour of the author's house or explore the rest of the farm on your own.

0.0	R	**Pleasant Valley Rd.**
1.7	S	**Garver Rd.**
3.9	R	**Oppossum Run Rd.**
4.1	L	**German Church Rd.**
5.9		Merge into **Belleville North**

Cume	Turn	Street/Landmark
8.2	L	**Riverside**
8.4	L	**Richland B&O Trail**
13.7	L	**95 East**
13.9	L	**Grant**—follow Rt. 95 signs
18.7	L	**SR 603**
19.1	L	**Pleasant Valley Rd.**
20.0	-	**Malabar Farm**
22.6		AngelWoods

A Valley View Inn, New Bedford, Ohio

A Valley View Inn

32327 State Route 643
New Bedford, OH 43824
Phone: (800) 331-VIEW (8439)
E-mail: valleyvu@bright.net
Web: www.ez-page.com/valleyview/
Innkeepers: Dan & Nancy Lembke
Rates: Budget to Moderate

> *Just get in your car & drive down the road,*
> *The closer you get, the lighter the load.*
> *And once you've been there, you'll visit again*
> *You see, I know a place called ...*
> *A Valley View Inn.*
> — from "I Know A Place," by Wes Bittenbender

Perched high on a ridge, with an outstanding view of an expansive valley, A Valley View Inn has incorporated a taste of Amish handiwork into its lodgings. Ohio has a large population of Amish, and the largest concentration is in this part of the state. Because the Amish use horse and buggies and bicycles as their primary means of transportation, the locals are respectful of slow-moving vehicles in the area—an obvious benefit to the touring cyclist as well.

The inn itself was built by an Amish man. Each of the ten rooms carry the colorful name of the quilt pattern used in that room: Alabama Star, Double Wedding Ring, Lone Star, Giant Dahlia, Log Cabin Broken Star, Sunflower on A Star, Broken Star, Star Song, Country Song Bird, and Country Lily label the doors. A beautiful armoire, rocking chair, blanket chest, quilt rack, and bed furnish each room, showcasing the local Amish talent, along with a small wall hanging that mimics the design of the bed quilt. A different color scheme distinguishes the similarly furnished and decorated rooms from one another. Each room has its own heating and air conditioning controls and a bath and shower combination—perfect for soaking after a day of challenging hills.

Quilting enthusiasts will marvel at the variety of quilts through-out the inn. In fact, groups of French quilters come to the inn each year for a marathon quilting bee and to gather fabric. Be-cause the quilts are works of art in and of themselves, always be sure to remove the quilt from your bed and hang it on the quilt rack to preserve the fabric.

As Nancy, the innkeeper, wants this to be a retreat for the body and soul, there is no TV to be found in the inn. However, the huge family room in the finished basement offers plenty of diver-sions, including games, player piano, a ping pong table, and darts. Of course, there is plenty of room for a large quilting bee. Outside there are 30 acres of property, with trails for hiking, a pond for fishing, and a porch, overlooking the valley, for relaxing. Binocu-lars are kept on hand for a closer look at the scenery in the distance. Closer at hand, the colorful gardens that Nancy has planted feature a wide variety of plants growing in the beds.

Breakfast is served in a large dining area, also furnished with locally-made dining sets. Nancy reads a devotion and invites guests to join in a prayer at the breakfast table. The French toast rates among the best I've ever tasted, and the fresh pineapple was a nice change from the traditional breakfast fruits.

Biking from A Valley View Inn
This very hilly area might surprise those who think of Ohio as one big, flat cornfield. The hills will test your quads and lungs. You'll pass through small towns, meeting horses and buggies along the way. Be sure to stop at Miller's Dutch Kitch'n in Bal-tic—the coconut cream pie is unsurpassed. A scenic train leaves from Sugar Creek and plenty of Amish home industries abound. Just remember that Amish businesses are closed on Sunday. Bakeries, furniture, and quilts are among the more popular prod-ucts enjoyed by the English, as all non-Amish are called. An Amishman behind a horse and plow is a common sight in the area, and you'll often see fresh laundry blowing in the breeze at many of the homes that you will pass. The Amish homes can be recognized by the lack of electrical wires, a modern convenience

forbidden by their religion and lifestyle which focuses on simpler, unmechanized ways. Certainly the ideal base for exploration of this interesting area is in the heart of the region, at A Valley View Inn.

Terrain: While there are a few flat stretches, the general trend is hilly.

Road Conditions: Watch for horse droppings in the road. Otherwise, the roads are reasonably well maintained.

Traffic: You will share the roads with other bikes, horses and buggies, and automobiles, but traffic is light.

Mountain Biking Opportunities: The many gravel roads in the area provide plenty of opportunities to explore.

Nearest Bike Shop
Countryside Bicycles
2012 Clark Township
Road 164
Sugarcreek, OH 44681
(330) 852-4949

A Valley View Inn to Baltic (25 miles)
You'll pass through several small towns including Sugar Creek and Baltic. Be sure to take some time off the bike to look around.

Cume	Turn	Street/Landmark
0.0	L	**SR 643**
2.5	S	New Bedford, continue on **SR 643**
6.3	L	**SR 643**
6.6	R	**SR 643** (Junction with 557)
7.9	L	**SR 93**
8.1	R	**CR 108**
8.7	-	**CR 108** becomes **CR 71**
10.5	R	**CR 72**
10.8	R	**Buckeye St. (CR 71)**

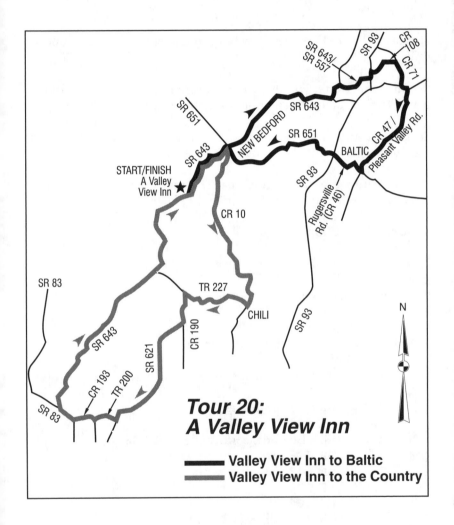

SR 643/
SR 557

SR 93

CR 108

CR 71

SR 651

SR 643

NEW BEDFORD

SR 643

SR 651

CR 47 /
Pleasant Valley Rd.

BALTIC

START/FINISH
A Valley
View Inn ★

CR 10

SR 93

Rugersville
Rd. (CR 46)

SR 83

TR 227

CHILI

N

SR 643

SR 93

CR 190

SR 83

SR 621

CR 193

TR 200

Tour 20:
A Valley View Inn

━━━ **Valley View Inn to Baltic**
▨▨▨ **Valley View Inn to the Country**

Cume	Turn	Street/Landmark
11.1	L	**Broadway**
11.4	R	**Main** (follow this out of town. It becomes **CR 47/ Pleasant Valley Rd.**)
17.5	R	**CR 46 (Ragersville Rd.)**
18.3	-	Begin steep hill into Baltic. Stop sign at bottom of fast descent.
18.6	S	Baltic; **CR 46** becomes **Main St.** Follow this out of town, becomes **SR 651**
22.5	L	**SR 643** (New Bedford town)
25.0	R	A Valley View Inn

A Valley View Inn to the Country (27.1 miles)

This road is really off the beaten track and in an unpopulated area. Be sure to stock up on water and supplies since Chili is about the only (and barely significant) town you'll pass through.

Cume	Turn	Street/Landmark
0.0	L	**SR 643**
2.5	R	**CR 10** (Follow to Chili)
8.1	R	**TR 227** (Chili)
10.3	L	**CR 190**
10.9	S	**CR 190** becomes **SR 621**
16.1	R	**TR 200**
16.9	R	**CR 193**
18.4	R	**SR 83** (no sign)
18.8	R	**SR 643**
27.1	L	A Valley View Inn

The Claire E, *a historic sternwheeler moored
in the Muskingum River in Marietta, Ohio*

Claire E Sternwheeler

Muskingum River
c/o 127 Ohio Street
Marietta, OH 45750
Phone: (740) 374-2233
Innkeeper: Harley Noland
Rates: Budget

> *If you come down to the river,*
> *Bet you gonna find some people who live.*
> *You don't have to worry 'cause you have no money,*
> *People on the river are happy to give.*

> — J.C. Fogerty, "Proud Mary"

At the confluence of the Muskingum and Ohio Rivers sits the town of Marietta, Ohio, a historic town that was the first permanent American settlement in the Northwest Territory and is currently home to the *Claire E*—the only sternwheeler B&B in the country.

Marietta—named in honor of Marie Antoinette—oozes history as well as charm. Museums, sternwheelers, and buildings from bygone eras adorn the landscape. The town has always taken advantage of both its historical and geographical position, and was an important connection on the Underground Railroad thanks to its location across the river from West Virginia. A short ride through town to view the grand old mansions is a pleasant way to pass an afternoon. The local tourist office can suggest enough activities in the area to keep you busy for several days.

It's easy to guess what the Marietta and the riverfront looked liked years ago when river vessels dominated the scene. Every year, the town remembers its proud past the weekend after Labor Day, when you'll be overwhelmed by the pageantry of the Sternwheel Festival. It definitely justifies a visit of several days. To begin your visit and for a great orientation to the town and its history, take a trolley tour. To see the town from the water and learn a bit about the rivers, hop aboard a sternwheeler that chugs up the river and gives a brief taste of river life.

But to best get a sense of the river, spend a few nights aboard the *Claire E*. The *Claire E* is definitely not your typical bed and breakfast. The vintage sternwheeler is listed on the National Register of Historic Maritime Vessels, and is moored away from the shore so that guests have the feeling of actually floating on the river rather than being permanently docked. Access to the sternwheeler involves a short trip on a raft—navigated by you—so you need to have a certain sense of adventure and be comfortable on the water. We visited just after a flood, when the water was swift and debris filled the space between the shore and the sternwheeler. Captain/Innkeeper Harley Noland had to add an additional telephone pole to his mooring because the water had risen so high. He will advise you of the river conditions if they might make your visit less than ideal, but keep in mind that situations like this occur only sporadically.

Harley comes from a long line of riverboat captains, so it wasn't surprising that he would someday find a boat and go a long way to get her. He located the *Claire E* in Alabama, about as far away as it could be from Marietta. Undaunted by the distance, he headed south, rebuilt the wheel, and returned with a new home. After all, sternwheelers are in his blood.

To lodge aboard the *Claire E*, you should feel comfortable in smaller surroundings. If you are on the upper deck, you will need to feel confident navigating a ladder to go up and down from your room. If you have any doubts, request the lower deck accommodation.

The vessel itself contains three bedrooms; the two on the upper deck share a bath. Since access to the bath is through a bedroom, Harley only rents out all four beds at a time on the upper deck to groups that are previously acquainted. Otherwise, only one of the rooms is rented, so if you would like the upper deck, you will have it to yourself without having to worry about strangers traipsing through your sleeping area. The beds are typical built-in berths.

On the main deck is a bedroom with a double iron bed and a private bath. A small dresser for your convenience fits into the snug little cabin. You'll feel the gentle current of the usually calm river, which will lull you to sleep. Don't expect your guestroom to be equipped or decorated like the QEII or one the Delta steamboats; this is a fun experience, and certainly casual.

In the common area you'll find newspaper articles about the *Claire E*, as well as photos of it in various states of restoration. At one time this vessel spent its life as a lowly push boat.

Harley no longer lives aboard the vessel, but has a boatsman run the operation. Harley is involved in several ventures, including the Levee House down on the Ohio River. Originally serving as a waiting area for riverboat passengers, the Levee House has been transformed into a wonderful restaurant with exhibits on the local history of the Underground Railroad. The trendy eatery features an extensive and varied menu offering something to suit the tastes of all patrons—we returned for several meals. Harley also runs the trolley and takes special interest groups on tours of local Underground Railroad sites.

Biking from the *Claire E*

Terrain: Located in the Appalachia region of southeastern Ohio, this area boasts hilly terrain that can be a challenge to the cyclist.

Road Conditions: The surfaces are in very good condition throughout both routes.

Traffic: It can get a little congested right in Marietta, but otherwise, traffic is light.

Mountain Biking Opportunities: The Wayne National Forest requires a permit for its many trails. Contact: Marietta Unit, Route 1, Box 132, Marietta, OH 45750, phone (740) 373-9055.

Nearest Bike Shop
Pedal Shop
404 Third Street
Marietta, OH 45750
Phone: (740) 374-8584

Coal Run Out and Back (33.8 miles)

Interspersed with the hills along this route, you'll pedal along the river much of the way to the village of Coal Run. Be sure to stop and see the hand-operated locks, the only ones of this kind still in existence in this country.

Cume	Turn	Street/Landmark
0.0	L	**Gilman**
0.6	L	**Pedestrian bridge** at Harmar Village, becomes **Butler St.**
0.9	L	**Front St.** (becomes **Rt. 60**)
2.3	L	**SR 60**
16.8	R	**Coal Run**; village here (turn around)
16.9	L	**SR 60**
22.6	R	**Lowell** (Lock #3 is to the left on Lock St.)
22.7	R	**SR 60** (Retrace your route back to the highway).
26.8	-	Nice uphill climb
28.1	-	**Devola**; Lock #2 is here
31.5	R	**Front St.**
32.9	R	**Butler St.** Keep right to pedestrian bridge, follow sign to Harmar Village
33.2	R	**Gilman**
33.8	R	*Claire E*

Hune House Out and Back (41.8 miles)

Here is another ride into the splendid countryside replete with nostalgic sites along the way. A covered bridge, a Mail Pouch barn, and the historic Hune House highlight this route. Be sure to take a tour of the Hune House and the artworks on display.

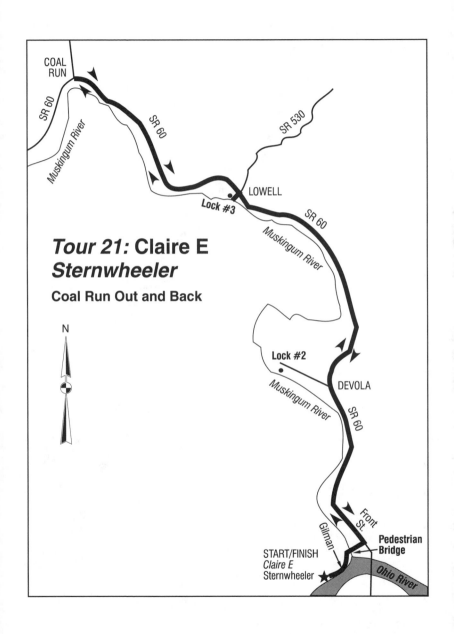

COAL
RUN

SR 60

Muskingum River

SR 60

SR 530

SR 60

LOWELL

Lock #3

Muskingum River

Tour 21: Claire E
Sternwheeler

Coal Run Out and Back

N

Lock #2

DEVOLA

Muskingum River

SR 60

Front St.

Gilman

Pedestrian
Bridge

START/FINISH
Claire E
Sternwheeler

Ohio River

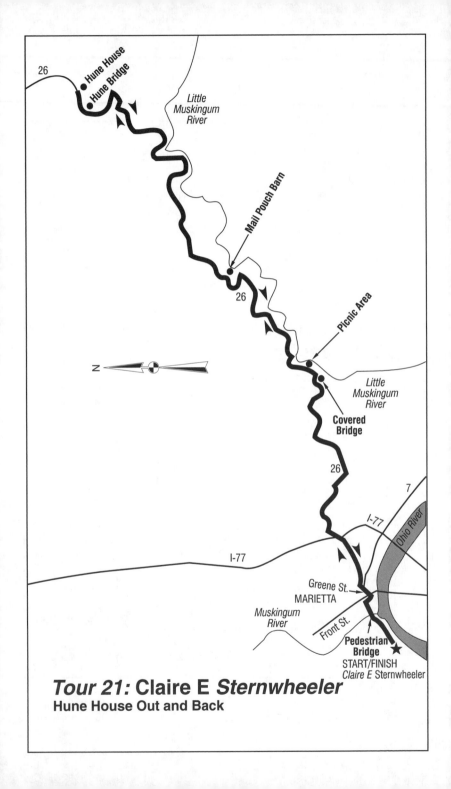

26

Hune House
Hune Bridge

*Little
Muskingum
River*

Mail Pouch Barn

26

Picnic Area

*Little
Muskingum
River*

**Covered
Bridge**

26

N

7

I-77

Ohio River

I-77

Greene St.
MARIETTA

*Muskingum
River*

Front St.

**Pedestrian
Bridge** ★
START/FINISH
Claire E Sternwheeler

Tour 21: **Claire E** *Sternwheeler*
Hune House Out and Back

Cume	Turn	Street/Landmark
0.0	L	**Gilman**
0.6	L	**Pedestrian bridge**
0.9	L	**Butler**
2.3	R	**Front**
2.5	L	**Greene**
3.0	L	**Rt. 26**
3.5	**BL**	Follow **Rt. 26**
9.1	-	Covered bridge
9.4	**BR**	**Rt. 26**; picnic area
13.5	-	Mail Pouch barn
20.8	-	Hune Bridge
20.9	**TA**	Hune House
32.4	**BL**	**Rt. 26**
38.3	**BR**	**Rt. 26**
38.8	R	**Greene**
39.3	R	**Front**
39.5	L	**Butler**
40.9	R	**Pedestrian Bridge**
41.2	R	**Gilman**
41.8	R	*Claire E*

The Cornerstone Inn, Archbold, Ohio

The Cornerstone Inn

300 West Street
Archbold, OH 43502
Phone: (419) 445-5340
Innkeepers: Jeff and Pat Borton
Rates: Budget to Moderate

"Nestling in the heart of one of the richest farming sections in the country, Archbold, Ohio, is typical of the best in American small towns. Orderly, well-tilled farms, neat fences, and freshly painted barns present a picturesque panorama spreading out from the village, hub of activity in the area. Here is the land that might have inspired the author of 'America the Beautiful' to write his 'amber waves of grain.' Here is a land of promise where milk and honey flow, especially milk." — From the *Edison News*, September 1949

Set in a perpetually thriving small town in the Northwestern part of the state, The Cornerstone Inn offers hospitality exceeded by none. The hosts, Pat and Jeff Borton, insist that you make this your home during your stay and encourage you to do exactly as you would at home. This includes helping yourself to the fridge and fixing yourself a beverage or a snack. This attention to their guests' comfort has earned them a reputation as the adopted family of many guests.

Archbold is the home base to many international companies, so many visitors from abroad come to the Cornerstone Inn while on contract in Archbold. This means that other guests have the unusual opportunity to mingle with the Europeans and Japanese who frequently stay here and, at the same time, test their foreign language skills.

As the name suggests, The Cornerstone Inn is a stone house that looks deceptively small from the outside. Once you step inside you will find that the space opens up and that there is room upon room within this homey structure. The Bortons reside in separate quarters in the basement, but they can be found socializing with the guests throughout the day. One very comfortable and cozy place for conversation is the den just off of the kitchen. Wicker furniture gives this multi-windowed area the feel of a summer home. The more formal living room has ample space for guests to relax and enjoy the fire. Like in many homes, though, the unofficial gathering place is the kitchen. This large room is set up perfectly to lean against the counters and pass the time talking with the other guests. A country dining room full of down-home accents extends the casual theme found throughout the inn.

The five bedrooms in the Cornerstone Inn are split between the two floors. On the first floor, the Barn Raisers Room gives a glimpse into the farmhouse style. Maroon, white, and green tones are used throughout to warm the natural hardwood floors. A border featuring primitive-style scenes complements the look. The room is furnished with a queen-sized bed, a large television, and for those with a sweet tooth, a dish of candy. The same color scheme extends into a private bathroom that contains nice fluffy linens.

Just across the hall is the Old Schoolhouse Room. If you guessed that an old school desk would be among the furnishings in this room, go to the head of the class. To complement the desk, there are school-related pictures on the walls. A queen bed and antique dresser round out the room, which is finished in a dark green and cream décor. There is also a large private bath.

On the second floor, you'll be delighted by Grandma's Attic, which has a cheery holiday feel. The dark green and berry wallpaper exudes a sense of well-being and relaxation. The day bed and white metal queen-size bed might have come straight from your own grandmother's attic. Hat boxes, a doll display, and white wicker furnishings are among the found treasures that furnish this room.

The Apple Core Room, located under the eaves, has windows in the alcove. The hardwood floors are covered by throw rugs. And like all good apple-themed rooms, the wallpaper is covered with designs based on the fruit, including a border of apples. The rocking chair provides a pleasant spot to lull yourself to sleep before having sweet apple dreams.

The largest of the rooms, the Quilters Corner Room, can accommodate four adults and one child. Two antique beds and an old hired hand's bed leave enough space for a separate seating area outfitted with a sofa and chairs. Scattered rugs cover parts of the natural floor, and handmade quilts hang from racks or on the walls. A variety of stuffed animals call this room home. Like all the rooms in The Cornerstone Inn, this room has a private bath, large television, and central air.

The Archbold area thrived even through the Great Depression. Mennonites settled the area long ago, and you will still find establishments that do not conduct business on Sundays. Besides the well-known La Choy plant, Sauders Furniture is also based in this quaint little town, and has an outlet store that is open to the public. What may be more interesting is Sauder Village. Located just outside of town, this living history village has 34 restored structures staffed with interpreters who demonstrate crafts and trades. In addition to the village attractions, there are also gifts, a quilt shop, and a bakery. Special exhibitions and events are planned from April through October and include such attractions as a fiddle contest, quilt shows, and apple butter making.

Biking from The Cornerstone Inn

Terrain: Flat.

Road Conditions: Good, paved roads.

Traffic: Light.

Mountain Biking Opportunities: The Wabash Canonball Rail Trail is nearby. For info visit www.toltbbs.com/~norta/index.htm.

Nearest Bike Shop
R Bike Shop
520 Clinton St
Defiance, OH 43512-2635
Phone: (419) 782-6756

The Cornerstone Inn to Harrison Lake State Park (41.6 miles)
This very flat route passes through large farms and Mennonite settlements. A great place to eat in Pettisville is the Das Essen Haus Restaurant, a Mennonite establishment where good home-cooked food is served. Harrison Lake State Park offers swimming, fishing, and hiking. Getting back closer to town, you will pass through Goll Woods, which has nature trails for exploration. A remnant of a prehistoric forest, this eerie primordial forest is a fine example of what the area probably looked like long ago. Be sure to lock your bike if you decide to stop and hike.

Cume	Turn	Street/Landmark
0.0	L	South
0.1	R	Defiance
1.1	R	D
4.8	L	19
11.0	L	K
11.5	L	L
18.5	R	26-1
19.5	L	M
20.3	L	27-1, becomes 21-1
28.5	L	I-25
28.8	BL	I-25 becomes F
32.7	R	24
34.7	L	D
35.8	R	Vine
41.1	R	Murbaugh
41.2	L	Defiance
41.5	L	South
41.6		Cornerstone Inn

A ride through the countryside (30.4 miles)
On this route, you'll cycle by huge farms and tiny villages. Stately churches rise from the fields as you approach small communities.

0.0	L	West
0.3	L	W. Barre, becomes C
7.2	R	Rt. 16
8.9	R	AC

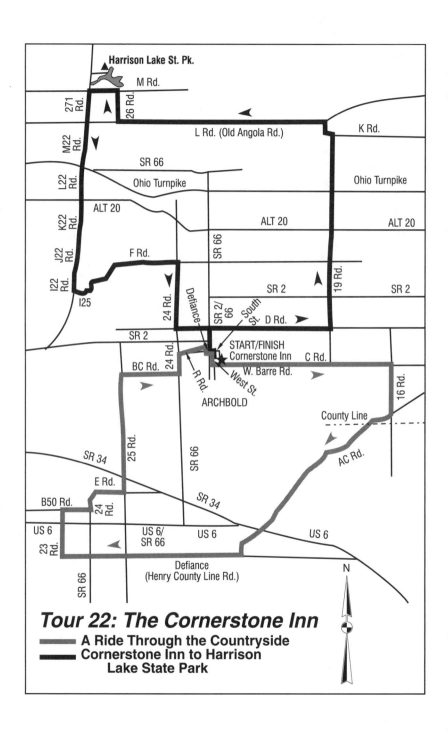

Harrison Lake St. Pk.

M Rd.

271 Rd.

26 Rd.

M22 Rd.

L Rd. (Old Angola Rd.)

K Rd.

SR 66

L22 Rd.

Ohio Turnpike

Ohio Turnpike

K22 Rd.

ALT 20

ALT 20

ALT 20

J22 Rd.

SR 66

F Rd.

SR 2

SR 2

19 Rd.

I22 Rd.

I25

24 Rd.

Defiance

SR 2/66

South St.

D Rd.

SR 2

START/FINISH
Cornerstone Inn

C Rd.

BC Rd.

24 Rd.

R Rd.

West St.

W. Barre Rd.

16 Rd.

ARCHBOLD

County Line

25 Rd.

SR 66

AC Rd.

SR 34

E Rd.

B50 Rd.

24 Rd.

SR 34

US 6

US 6/
SR 66

US 6

US 6

23 Rd.

SR 66

Defiance
(Henry County Line Rd.)

N

Tour 22: The Cornerstone Inn

A Ride Through the Countryside
**Cornerstone Inn to Harrison
Lake State Park**

Cume	Turn	Street/Landmark
15.9	R	**Defiance** (Henry County)
20.1	R	**23** (Be careful to get on the correct 23—there is another in the other county)
21.4	R	**B50**
22.3	L	**24**
23.1	R	**E**
23.9	L	**25**
27.3	R	**BC**
28.3	L	**24**
29.2	R	**R**
30.2	R	**Defiance**
30.3	L	**South**
30.4		Cornerstone Inn

The Greenhouse

47 East 5ᵗʰ Street
Chillicothe, OH 45601
Phone: (740) 775-5313
Innkeepers: Dee and Tom Shoemaker
Rates: Budget

Love your life, perfect your life, beautify all things in your life. Seek to make your life long and its purpose in the service of your people. — Chief Tecumseh

Chillicothe was one of the first towns west of the Alleghenies to be settled. It became the first state capital of Ohio, and was home to the Shawnee tribe lead by Chief Tecumseh. Before the Shawnees arrived, the ancient Hopewell peoples inhabited this area. Mounds can be viewed at the Hopewell Culture National Historic Park, just north of town. To commemorate its past history, Chillicothe presents the outdoor drama *Tecumseh!* from late June to early September. This event portrays the life and times of the Shawnee tribe and early settlers to the area.

Set in a valley along the Scioto River, Chillicothe is located on the Appalachian escarpment and is surrounded by hills, a prominent feature of the area and the inspiration for the Great Seal of the State of Ohio. To preserve this view, a state park, aptly named Great Seal State Park, was established.

Today, Chillicothe maintains a dignified air, thanks to the preservation of many of the area's historic sites. Adena, the home of Thomas Worthington, an early Ohio governor, is open for public viewing. Right in town, the First Capital District possesses a variety of buildings from the early 1800s that merit a view.

Another notable building is The Greenhouse Bed and Breakfast. A huge wrap-around porch hints at the enormity of this Queen Anne-style house, built circa 1894. Listed on the National Register of Historic Places, The Greenhouse displays the opulence of another era. If you can resist the temptation to simply plop yourself down on the front porch and relax, you will be escorted through the home by Dee Shoemaker, known at the tourist office as "Ms. Hospitality." Massive leaded glass hardwood doors open into the equally large entryway, where you eyes will fix on the majestic imported Italian fireplace. Surrounding the fireplace, Dee's collections give the illusion that you have entered an antiques shop. She collects multiples of the same object, grouping them together in menageries throughout the house. But you won't feel like the proverbial bull in the china shop as this place has room to roam.

The first floor boasts several opulent yet comfortable rooms for relaxation. The fine handiwork in these rooms speaks volumes of the skilled craftsmen who created this marvelous place. Chandeliers, oak and cherry woodwork, inlaid floors, and ornate ceilings reflect the grand manner and extra attention to detail found in homes of this period.

One could literally spend hours examining and admiring the special embellishments that adorn these gathering spaces. The comfortable chairs and other antique furnishings throughout the home are perfectly matched to the period of the home. Besides the fireplace in the entryway, there are several others found throughout this exquisite mansion.

The dining room graciously occupies the immense turret, providing an abundance of light and giving the room a rather interesting shape. A huge table, fit for a king, complements the antique buffet. One interesting feature in this room is a butler call button; Dee insists it is not there to summon her husband Tom to perform his duties.

On our visit—a rather hot and humid day—Dee welcomed us with a cold beverage and freshly baked cookies. She immediately lived up to the title bestowed upon her by the tourism office. The central air comforted us, and Dee insisted we go to our room with our refreshments to relax a bit before starting our cycling adventure.

A grand staircase leads to the second floor, which offers four spacious retreats—all with private baths—to guests. Our room, in the back of the house, occupied a turret, with huge windows to provide an abundance of light. The antique wood bed rests in the curve of the turret and seems insignificant within this immense room. An armoire stands next to the bed, and a desk, dresser, antique chairs, and another armoire can be found elsewhere in the room. Along plate rails, a collection of blue granite dishes encircles the room. A crystal chandelier provides additional lighting.

Facing the front of the house, another large bedroom, decorated in mauve, blue, and green holds an antique tester bed. Light flows through two huge windows and an attractive, oval stained glass window. The blue floral wallpaper contrasts sharply with the bright white mantel of the fireplace. An armoire, fainting sofa, wooden doll furniture, a sewing machine and antique collectables fill the room.

Next door, an equally large guestroom contains three twin beds, a perfect setup for friends traveling together. The walls of this room are beige with a border. A blue and white fireplace fits well into the blue and beige color scheme used throughout. Wicker and wooden chairs provide seating, and two mirrored dressers offer plenty of space for unpacking. A portrait of George Washington hangs on the wall, as do a variety of cups—yet another of Dee's collections.

The fourth bedroom reflects a lifestyle from the past. A pie keeper and an old washing tub remind one of the days before mechanization. Floral chairs, an antique trunk, dresser, and armoire are scattered about the room. The queen-size fourposter spindle bed and the yellow fireplace with a white mantel fit wonderfully into the scheme of this room. The private bath for this room is located across the hall.

Biking from The Greenhouse

The biking in this area is obviously demanding. The mix of open spaces and towering hills make for ideal cycling if you enjoy constant ups and downs. The view from the tops of the ridges are marvelous; in fact, it is said that Columbus can be seen on a clear day. Because some of the roads are older, they are steep and inconsistently graded. The downhills are fast and give some momentum to attack the next hill. Parks and pull-outs along the routes make excellent rest stops. This area might remind you of Vermont, and is certainly an area that I like to recommend to those who think that Ohio is flat.

Terrain: Hilly except for right in town.

Road Conditions: Generally good, with shoulders on busier stretches.

Traffic: Light to moderate.

Mountain Biking Opportunities: Scioto Trail State Forest,124 North Ridge Road, Waverly, OH 44690-9513, (740) 663-2523. The bike shop below can offer trail advice.

Nearest Bike Shop

Just North Of Daytona
51 East Main Street
Chillicothe, OH 45601-2504
Phone: (740) 775-7873

The Greenhouse to the Hills (20.0 miles)

Almost as soon as you cross the river, you'll start winding and climbing. The views are great—and so are the downhills. Do keep alert when coming downhill, as stop signs seemed inconveniently placed midway down.

Cume	Turn	Street/Landmark
0.0	L	Fifth
0.5	L	Bridge
0.7	R	Main

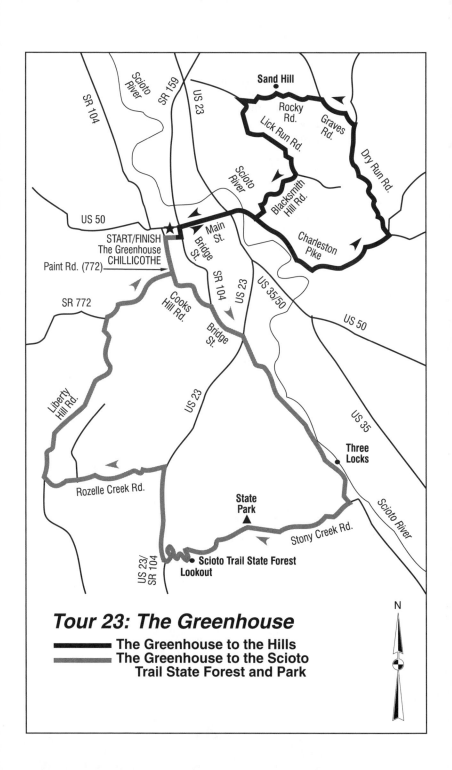

Tour 23: The Greenhouse

▬▬▬ The Greenhouse to the Hills
░░░ The Greenhouse to the Scioto
Trail State Forest and Park

N

Cume	Turn	Street/Landmark
2.5	S	**Charleston Pike**
6.8	L	**Dry Run** (no sign—church cemetery on corner)
9.7	L	**Graves**
10.6	L	**Rocky**
11.5	-	Hill to mile 12.0
13.1	L	**Lick Run**
15.6	R	**Blacksmith Hill**
17.4	R	**Charleston**; becomes **Main**
19.7	L	**Paint**
19.9	L	**Fifth**
20.0		Greenhouse

The Greenhouse to the Scioto Trail State Forest and Park (26.7 miles)

Get ready for some more hills. Scioto Trail has a great position high in the hills, and a picnic area is available. The climb up will require some effort, but returning to Chillicothe takes little more than keeping your hands on the brakes in preparation for stops.

0.0	R	**Caldwell**
0.3	R	**E. 8**th
0.4	L	**Paint (Rt. 772)**
0.9	L	**Cooks Hill**
1.3	R	**Bridge St./S 104**; no sign, use shoulder
2.6	-	Interchange
7.6	R	**Stoney Creek Rd.** (Three Locks sign)
13.4	R	**US 23, Rt. 104**
15.7	L	**Rozelle Creek Rd.**
15.9	BR	At Y
18.9	R	**Liberty Hill**
23.8	R	**Rt. 772**, becomes **Paint**
26.6	R	**Fifth**
26.7		The Greenhouse

The Inn at Brandywine Falls

8230 Brandywine Road
Sagamore Hills, OH 44067-2810
Phone: (216) 467-1812, (216) 650-4965
Innkeepers: George and Katie Hoy
Rates: Moderate to Luxury

> *"They live at the Inn*
> *so our entrees, of course,*
> *do not include goat,*
> *our own chickens, or horse."*

— George and Katie Hoy, *Inn Good Taste*

The above ditty provides a peek into the humor you'll enjoy at The Inn at Brandywine Falls. George and Katie Hoy have written a book that gives a glimpse into the lives of innkeepers and their guests, and provides a wonderful sample of the recipes served at the inn. *Inn Good Taste* and a guest information booklet are found in each room and provide interesting reading, sprinkled with generous portions of the innkeepers' characteristic humor. Of course, even better than reading the humorous stories is hearing them firsthand and enjoying the company of your hosts.

A perfect place to base yourself for your adventure, the converted farmstead and expansive grounds of the Inn at Brandywine Falls is set on a ridge within the boundaries of the Cuyahoga Valley National Recreation Area (CVRNA). Very popular with those celebrating special occasions, this retreat attracts the majority of its guests from within a forty-mile radius. So inviting is the inn that even the neighbor drives over twice a year to enjoy a getaway. Those of you beyond the forty-mile radius will find the distance insignificant when weighed against the benefits.

The main house, which is on the National Register of Historic Places, has four sleeping rooms. On the first floor, the James Wallace Parlour (named for the prosperous former mill owners who lived here) faces the front and has a private exit to an inviting porch. A fireplace, sleigh bed, and comfortable chair and foot-stool grace the room. Done in pale yellow with an Axminster carpet and a woven 1844 coverlet on the bed, the room is large and relaxing. The painted window shades depict local scenes.

Upstairs, Adeline's Retreat offers a somewhat feminine touch. A sleigh bed, painted floor, and white armchair blend perfectly with the subtle dove gray walls to create a welcoming and intimate space. The Victorian-style bath features antique fixtures and a clawfoot tub.

Anna Hale's Garrett, a two-room suite under the eaves, has a small sleeping room with two cannonball beds. The anteroom has two studio beds, a desk, and a toy theme. The sloping ceilings cozy up the space but aren't recommended for the very tall. The bath contains an interesting vanity—double sinks in a dresser.

Offering a light and airy appearance, the Simon Perkins Room contains two double fourposter beds; a coral and green border surrounds the room. The light blue color scheme sets the tone for the Ohio theme prevalent in the wall décor. The star quilts and white ruffle around the beds complete the look. A pedestal sink and a quilt used as a shower curtain accent the bathroom.

The common areas include a large living room, a dining room, and a library. The library has quite a collection of books, including a scrapbook documenting the renovation of the inn. The large dining room has a sideboard and a green tole-painted table where you will enjoy the sumptuous breakfast served by your hosts. Freshly baked bread, oatmeal soup, and a special entrée fuel you for the day. Be sure to ask about the Zone diet.

The living room, with a fireplace, is a perfect place to curl up and read or visit with other guests. A piano awaits those inclined to entertain. Best of all is the inviting porch—sit a spell and enjoy the surroundings.

For those desiring seclusion, there is a separate structure out back with two large two-story retreats—the Loft and the Granary. Both overlook a hemlock grove and retain the original rustic décor, with wide-plank floors and exposed hand-hewn beams. Modern amenities include a Jacuzzi, microwave, small refrigerator, and the makings for coffee and tea. The main floors have a living and dining area, and the upstairs lofts each contain a king bed. Breakfast can be served in your suite if you prefer. Antique farm implements grace the walls.

The Hoys have plans to open another inn within the boundaries of the CVRNA. Given the wonderful job they have done with this house, you can expect that the new inn to be just as remarkable.

Cycling from The Inn at Brandywine

I recall the first time I reluctantly visited the Cuyahoga Valley. A local cycling group had planned a weekend of camaraderie with options for canoeing, hiking, and of course, bicycling. Noticing the obvious elation of certain participants, I withheld my reservations about the prospects for excitement to be found so near a large urban area like Cleveland. Having lived the majority of my life in Ohio, I couldn't imagine what the big deal about this place was.

Fortunately for me, I never made my thoughts known. I was totally shocked and very pleased with this wonderful retreat, so near an urban area and yet so removed. I have returned several times and wholeheartedly extol the virtues of this natural showplace. With towpaths, hike-bike trails, and the Emerald Necklace of the Cleveland Metroparks available, one could spend great quantities of time exploring the region year-round. The visitors centers, historic exhibits, Hale Farm, a trip on the railroad, or a concert at the nearby Blossom Music Center are great places to spend some time. Plan on a leisurely pace to enjoy all this area has to offer.

Terrain: The inn itself sits high on a ridge, so if you stay on the ridge, you won't find drastic elevation changes. However, the two rides below do descend into the valley, which is very pleasant and exhilarating. Getting out of the valley is another story, which means climbing. But if you aren't keen on climbing, there are plenty of places to park your car and start the rides down in the valley.

Road Conditions: Part of the routes use trails, which are hard-packed crushed stone. Most of the roads are good, with the exception of Stanford Road, which is closed to vehicular traffic and not maintained. Potholes and debris cover the road on this section.

Traffic: Pathway traffic may be heavy on weekends, and road traffic is light.

Mountain Biking Opportunities: The Bike and Hike trails offer plenty of miles of off-road opportunities. Thick gravel and steep descents that intersect with roadways require caution.

Points of Interest: The CVRNA is full of exhibits, picnic areas, geological features, hiking trails, and other activities.

Bike Shops
Eddy's Bike Shop
3707 Darrow Road
Stow, OH 44224-4011
Phone: (330) 688-5521

The Inn at Brandywine to South Trail Terminus (25.1 miles)
This route goes through Peninsula, where you can board an excursion train or stop for lunch. As the trail follows the old canal bed, it passes near the Cuyahoga River.

Cume	Turn	Street/Landmark
0.0	R	**Brandywine Rd.**
0.5	R	**Metroparks Bike and Hike Trail**
4.1	R	Get off the trail here (milepost 10) before the overpass. Go through the **parking lot** of the Budget Inn and Wagon Wheel Restaurant to the road
4.2	R	**Old 8**
4.4	L	**Rt. 303**; Streetsborough
7.4	R	**N. Locust** (traffic light). Town of Peninsula

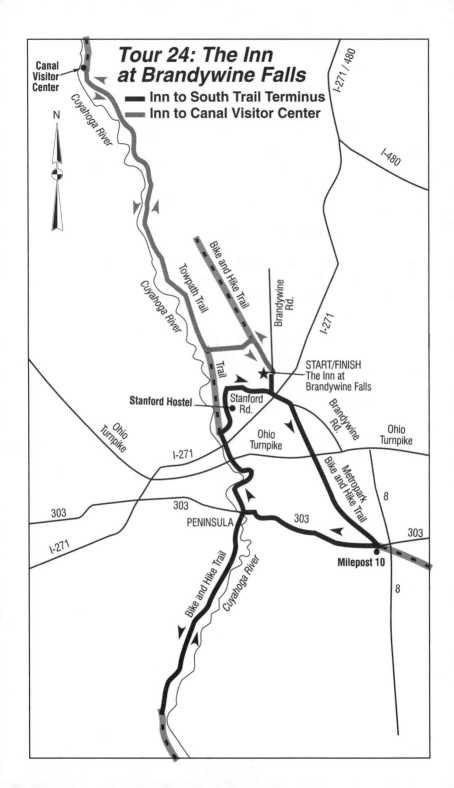

Cume	Turn	Street/Landmark
7.5	L	**W. Mill St.**
7.6	L	Into **parking area**
7.7	L	Onto **trail** (you will go up and cross a bridge)
14.1	TA	Back on **trail**
23.3	R	Short **path** that goes to Stanford Hostel
23.5	L	**Stanford Rd.**
24.5	-	Rough road begins, go around barricades
25.0	L	**Brandywine Rd.**
25.1	L	Inn at Brandywine

Inn at Brandywine to Canal Visitor Center (17.6 miles)
This route goes in the opposite direction of the first. It passes through several metroparks and past historic buildings that are open to visitors.

0.0	L	**Brandywine Rd.**
0.3	L	**Bike and Hike Trail**
1.0	L	**Highland Rd.**
2.0	R	**Towpath Trail**
8.8	TA	Lock Visitor Center
15.6	L	**Highland**
16.6	R	**Hike and Bike Trail**
17.3	R	**Brandywine**
17.6	R	Inn

The Ivy House

504 Ottawa Street
Marblehead, OH 43440
Phone: (419) 798-4944; (419) 798-9361
Innkeepers: Susan and Ray Lawyer
Rates: Budget; second night and weekday discounts available

"Just opposite, an island of the sea,
There came enchantment with the shifting wind,"
— John Keats, "Hyperion"

A finger jutting into Lake Erie, the Marblehead Peninsula derives its name from the expansive quarries located here. Though some are still in operation, many are now gone. Thanks to the beautiful lakeside setting, tourism has kept the local economy from skipping a beat. Taking full advantage of this ideal location, the Ivy House lives up to both its name and brochure description—simplicity and ivy. Decorated inside and out with an ivy theme, the cottage ambience sets the mood for informal relaxation. Ivy House has shared bathrooms; one on each floor. Rooms are smaller but offer ample space and good mattresses.

The approach to the Ivy House is via a short gravel lane. The natural woodland setting of the inn—formerly the home of a sea captain—conjures up memories of visits to a favorite family cottage. Grandma doesn't greet you at the door with treats, but you might find a snack waiting on the table along with hot or cold drinks that are always available.

You will enter Ivy House through a screened-in porch, where you can wile away the time relaxing after a ride, reading, visiting with other guests, or simply enjoying the peace and quiet. Proceeding into the living area, you'll find comfortable green wicker furniture beneath a ceiling fan that diffuses the fresh breezes off Lake Erie. Binoculars are available for scanning the view. If this isn't entertainment enough, you can always resort to watching something on the TV and VCR.

At the other end of the living area is the dining area, featuring a white trellis that covers the walls and ceilings; there's also an ivy border. Breakfast here is a treat—innkeeper Susan Lawyer bakes extra coffeecakes and wraps them up for guests to take home.

The two bedrooms are located in opposite corners of the first floor. Tucked under the eaves, the Pansy Room has a rustic theme with its barn siding, an ivy border, and simple coverings over the windows that face the lake. An in-room sink is an added convenience.

The bathroom, shared with the Geranium Room down the hall, contains an old clawfoot tub and shower. The room is outfitted just like your bathroom at home, with most toiletries, a heating pad, and even a hair dryer. The tub is surrounded by a pillow ticking curtain, and the sink is also skirted.

In the opposite corner of the first floor is the bright and cheerful Geranium Room, which is outfitted with both a queen and a twin bed. There is red carpet on the floors and floral stencils on the white walls. Two robes for the short trek to the bathroom hang in the closet. A ceiling fan cools the room.

Upstairs, three more bedrooms offer a variety of sleeping options. At the top of the stairs, the Dahlia Room, with its white wood plank floor and rose throw rugs, contains a double bed. Ivy designs are stenciled on the white walls. This room adjoins the Daisy Room, which has twin trundles and an in-room sink. A gray plank floor and paneling are accented with a floral border, blue blinds, and a blue-and-white eyelet valance. These two rooms may be rented together as a suite and are ideal for families or friends traveling together who prefer separate space.

The Ivy Room, the largest in the house, also has a gray plank floor with scattered throw rugs. White and pink tulle fabric draped above the queen bed lends a romantic touch to the white-paneled room. An antique dresser with an oval mirror, a rocker, and twin trundle beds complete the furnishings. Though this room shares the hallway bath (containing a shower and the same nice selection of toiletries that are also found downstairs), it is equipped with its own in-room sink.

The mellow, soothing atmosphere of this house—not to mention the discounts available to groups that rent the whole house or guests that stay a second night—make this a perfect retreat for a family, cycling group, or bunch of friends. Guests even have privileges at a nearby private beach resort.

Susan and Ray Lawyer are the hosts, and they live off the premises. Susan can direct you to anything you need, and is happy to engage you in conversation at breakfast. A retired English teacher, she now takes a keen interest in local politics and her community and can give you all the behind-the-scenes details.

Biking from The Ivy House

Bicycle touring around this resort area exposes you to the past. Right next door is the Lakeside Chautauqua—an area of summer cottages, shops, concerts, and a beach. Johnson's Island housed an officers' prisoner of war camp during the Civil War; a short detour over a causeway leads to the cemetery and monument. Other historic spots of note are the Wolcott House and the Marblehead lighthouse, the longest continuously-operating lighthouse on the Great Lakes. Of natural significance is the Lakeside Daisy Refuge; in spring you can see these rare specimens, which occur naturally only here and in two other places in the world. You'll also see the remains of several quarries—and some that are still in operation—around this peninsula.

Cedar Point, the amusement park renowned for its outstanding roller coasters, is nearby; a ferry leaves from Lakeside on certain days. You'll catch a glimpse of the ride skeletons as you cruise around the peninsula. East Harbor State Park, the largest in Ohio, offers a nice swimming beach as well as a picnic area.

A short ferry ride takes you to the largest American island in Lake Erie. Kelley's Island is a low-key resort area that boasts the Glacial Grooves, a fine example of the effects of retreating glaciers. A petroglyphic rock can also be viewed near the ferry dock. Kelley's Island is a fun place to spend an entire day, with bicycling, butterflies, ship watching, and relaxing. The state park has a beach for swimming, while the downtown area offers shops and restaurants for your browsing and dining pleasure

Terrain: Because they are basically flat, both of these rides are perfect for beginners.

Road Conditions: All roads are paved.

Traffic: On Kelley's Island the traffic is minimal, as most choose to ride bicycles or rent golf carts. On the mainland, traffic can get hectic on summer weekends and holidays.

Mountain Biking: A very short stretch of abandoned railroad bed runs nearby, and the Resthaven area across the bay has good mountain biking. Susan can give you details and directions. You can also ride at Castalia Quarry, though you'll need a permit. Call Erie County Metro Parks at (419) 625-7783.

Nearest Bike Shop
Bike Rack
3005 West Monroe Street
Sandusky, OH 44870-1812
Phone: (419) 625-3399

Kelleys Island (9.5 miles)
The island is a relaxed, delightful place. It is virtually impossible to get lost; just turn down whichever roads you like if you prefer to explore on your own. The island is so compact that a dead-end or wrong turn won't rack up the mileage. The following route basically circumnavigates the island.

Cume	Turn	Street/Landmark
0.0	L	Prairie
0.1	R	Frances
0.3	L	SR 163

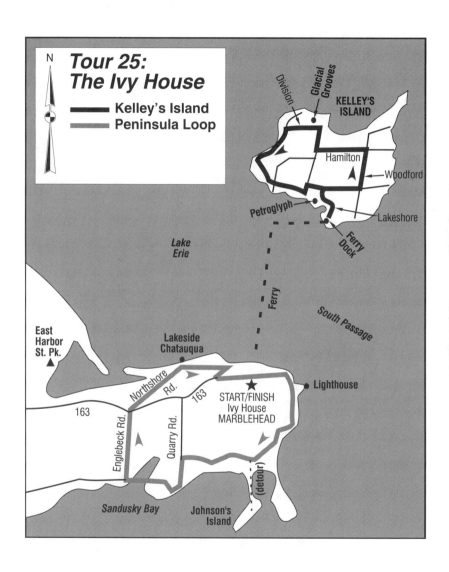

N

**Tour 25:
The Ivy House**

━━━ Kelley's Island
━━━ Peninsula Loop

Division

Glacial
Grooves

**KELLEY'S
ISLAND**

Hamilton

Woodford

Petroglyph

Lakeshore

Ferry
Dock

*Lake
Erie*

Ferry

South Passage

**East
Harbor
St. Pk.**

**Lakeside
Chatauqua**

Northshore

Rd.

163

★
START/FINISH
Ivy House
MARBLEHEAD

● Lighthouse

163

Englebeck Rd.

Quarry Rd.

(detour)

Sandusky Bay

**Johnson's
Island**

Cume	Turn	Street/Landmark
0.6	L	**Ferry Dock**. (*Note:* when leaving the ferry, follow traffic and bear right onto **Lakeshore**
2.0	L	**Woodford**
2.2	R	**Monaghan**
3.0	L	**Hamilton**
4.1	R	**Division**
4.8	-	Glacial Grooves. Exit parking lot and make a quick right on **Division** and a quick right on **Titus**
8.3	L	**Division**
8.8	-	**Ferry Dock**
9.1	R	**SR 163**
9.3	R	**Frances**
9.4	L	**Prairie**
9.5	R	Ivy House

Peninsula Loop (12.6 miles)

The ride is short, but the attractions are many. Be sure to stop at the lighthouse, Johnson Island, and Lakeside Chautauqua. Throughout the summer there are many concerts and lectures from which to choose. There is a small gate fee, but that permits access to the beach and use of all facilities within the grounds.

0.0	L	**Prairie**
0.1	R	**Frances**
0.2	L	**SR 163**
3.3	-	Detour to Johnson Island
4.7	BL	**Quarry**
6.4	R	**Englebeck**
8.0	S	**Northshore** will become **5th**; entrance to Lakeside
11.2	L	**Walnut**
11.5	R	**E. 2nd**
12.0	BL	**Prairie**
12.6	L	**Ottawa St.**—Ivy House

Liberty House

208 North Detroit
US Route 68
West Liberty, OH 43357-0673
Phone: (800) 437-8109, (937) 465-1101
E-mail: wrpent@loganrec.com
Web: www.libertyhousebandb.com/
Innkeepers: Sue and Russ Peterson
Rates: Budget

Let us think of Mother Earth, her rich bounty that will result from springtime, the golden corn and the seeds of harvest, all grown strong from Mother Earth, the spring rains, and the energy of Father Sky. It is time to consider healing: healing of ourselves, healing of a loved one, healing of adversaries for peace among nations, and healing of the harms done to Mother Earth.
— A contemporary rendition of an Indian prayer

The Shawnee Indians referred to this area in the Mad River Valley as *mac a chee*, meaning "smiling valley." This reference still holds true; the near perfect combination of biking and hospitality will bring a smile to your face. Although we biked the routes in a torrential downpour, the pastoral scenery and the historical landmarks along the way were able to take our minds off the drenching rain.

Small town living in a grand style succinctly describes the Liberty House, which takes a stately position along the main street of West Liberty, Ohio. Russ and Sue Peterson, the hosts, have done an outstanding job of decorating their inn and emphasizing its many unique features. The beige Victorian, trimmed in green, is surrounded by a wraparound porch, complete with a swing near the entry. A grand variety of plants and flowers surround the perimeter of the house and yard. Landscaping like this gets the gardening juices flowing, inspiring even those among us without green thumbs to dig up the yard and plant some flowers.

In the front parlor, which serves as the reception area, there are plenty of brochures with information on the many local attractions. A resident cat wanders throughout the house, but doesn't mind guests. Just inside the doorway is an umbrella stand— much appreciated by cyclists who always diligently pack their raingear, but don't necessarily think about carrying an umbrella for on-foot exploration in inclement weather.

The formal living room, connected to the parlor, has beautiful, patterned oak floors and natural woodworking that managed to escaped the wrath of the white brush when painted woodwork became popular. Antique furnishings accumulated by the Petersons over the years set the tone for the decorating scheme throughout the house.

Beyond the staircase is the large dining room; it, too, is furnished with antiques and has a patterned floor. Guests are served breakfast at an enormous table on fine china. Sue changes the pattern on a daily basis, thus giving you the chance to sample her collection.

The Masters Room is very grand and opulent, furnished and decorated much like you might expect for the head of the house. Empire-style furnishings and many antiques convey a sense of power to these very attractive quarters. The hallway bath is shared with the adjoining room.

The Teal Room, where we stayed, has two beds: a queen and a twin. We especially liked the nice, crisp linen spreads on the beds. Sue collects antique linens, and the freshly ironed bed linens are a sensual treat. There is a large closet for storage and plenty of space for sitting, writing letters, or just relaxing. Windows are covered in lacey curtains and little accoutrements are scattered throughout the room. A tapestry rocker is perfect for a soothing rest, with a ceiling fan above cooling the air.

The Teal Room and The Masters Room share a bathroom. The heat lamp installed there warmed us up after a long and wet ride. Toiletries are thoughtfully provided for guests.

Just outside of the guestrooms is a small sitting room with a plantation desk, comfy chairs, and a spinning wheel. A small refrigerator stores cold refreshments.

Downstairs, the Petersons' private bedroom may be rented when needed. The bathroom is a huge and wonderful place; an old storage area has been converted into a spacious bathing retreat.

The Liberty House was spotlessly clean with a décor both subtle and elegant. Many of the features compare favorably with those offered by pricier inns. For this reason, and because of the charms of the surrounding area, we feel that this is an exceptional lodging and cycling value.

Biking from Liberty House
Not far from Liberty House is Campbell Hill, the highest point in Ohio at 1533 feet. It is also the highest point between the Alleghenies and the Rockies; it's surprising that the state's high point isn't in the Appalachian region in the southeastern part of Ohio. Regardless, it might feel like you've climbed to the top of the state once you pedal up CR 10 in the Zanesfield loop below. Besides the hills and the expansive vistas that come with them, other points of interest along the way include the Piatt Castles, Underground Railroad sites, and the Zanesfield Shawnee Caverns. Nearby Bellefontaine claims the first concrete road in the country, as well as the shortest street in the world—a mere 17 feet.

Terrain: The area offers diverse terrain, varying from flat to very hilly.

Road Conditions: All roads are paved and in good condition.

Traffic: These back roads carry little traffic.

Nearest Bike Shop
Pedal Power Bicycle Shop
114 S. Detroit St.
West Liberty, Ohio 43357
Phone: (937) 465-6525

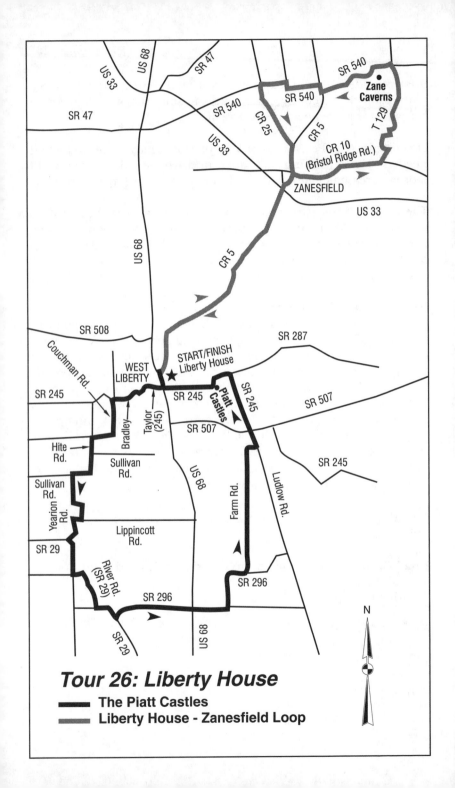

Tour 26: Liberty House

▬▬▬ **The Piatt Castles**
▨▨▨ **Liberty House - Zanesfield Loop**

The Piatt Castles (24.8 miles)

This ride has some rolling hills and passes many farms and the Piatt Castles. These imposing structures, owned by two brothers, are built from native limestone and are lavishly decorated. They are worth a stop, even if only for the novelty of visiting a castle in Ohio.

Part of this tour follows the route that the local bike shop uses for the organized ride that it sponsors every year. You might see some of the arrow markings along the way.

Cume	Turn	Street/Landmark
0.0	**R**	**N. Detroit**
0.1	**R**	**Baird**
0.5	**L**	**Taylor** (*Note:* this and next two directions follow **Rt. 245**)
0.6	**R**	**Runkle**
0.8	**L**	**Bradley**
1.9	**L**	**Couchman**
3.7	**L**	**Hite**
4.2	**L/R**	jog **Sullivan**
5.2	**R**	**Yearian**
6.9	**R**	**Lippincott**
7.7	**L**	**River (Rt. 29)**
8.8	**BL**	Follow **Rt. 29**
10.1	**BL**	Follow **Rt. 29** (stop sign here)
10.9	**L**	**296**
13.2	**S**	*Caution* crossing Rt. 68
14.3	**L**	**296**
15.4	**BR**	**296**
16.1	**S**	**Farm Rd.**
19.9	**L**	**Ludlow**
22.4	**L**	**Rt. 245** (Piatt Castles on this road)
24.6	**R**	**Alley**
24.8	**R**	Liberty House

Liberty House-Zanesfield Loop (29.9 miles)

Be prepared for some steep climbs on this ride. This route includes remnants of a marked cycling route (several signs are still in place) by the Ohio Department of Transportation. Zanesfield has services, and you'll pass by the Zanesfield Shawnee Caverns. The scenery is truly spectacular. Coming off the ridge, you'll attain high speeds, so exercise caution.

Cume	Turn	Street/Landmark
0.0	L	**S. Detroit**
0.5	R	**CR 5**
7.6	R	**CR 5** (Water St. Junction) Zanesfield
8.0	R	**CR 10 (Bristol Ridge)**. Steep 1.2 mile climb, then gradual for 1.2 miles
11.0	L	**Perry Township Rd. 129**
14.5	L	**SR 540** (Watch for Zanesfield Shawnee Caverns on your left in about 1.5 miles)
16.9	R	**SR 540**
17.0	L	**SR 540**
19.0	L	**CR 25**
21.2	R	**CR 5** (CR 25 ends)
22.3	L	**CR 5** (Water St. Junction) Zanesfield
29.4	L	**S. Detroit**
29.9	R	Liberty House

The Mill House

24070 Front Street
P.O. Box 102
Grand Rapids, OH 43522
Phone: (419) 832-6455
E-mail: innkeeper@themillhouse.com
Web: www.themillhouse.com
Innkeepers: Marsha and Dave Frost
Rates: Budget to Moderate

There is a large amount of bicycle touring this fall. The weather is cooler and there are good paths along the river roads: while the autumn scenery is beautiful in the extreme, it is becoming well-known that Mr. Hunter of the Commercial House makes special prices to wheeling parties, and he gets about all that pass this way. — Tri-County Bulletin, October 19, 1897

A hundred years have passed since the above quote appeared in the local paper. The Commercial House no longer exists, but the cycling remains the same. Once a part of the Great Black Swamp—a dark, hostile environment rampant with disease, full of wild animals, snakes, and mosquitoes—northwestern Ohio was literally drained by enterprising settlers. From this murk arose the fertile farmlands through which you will cycle.

Grand Rapids, a sleepy village on the Miami-Erie Canal, entices its visitors with myriad activities: shopping in those quaint little places you never see at home, visiting the Ludwig Mill, riding a canal boat, or admiring the historic buildings.

One such building is the Mill House. Located on the main street and backing up to the river, it originally housed the steam-powered Stump's Mill, a structure that deteriorated after milling operations ceased in the 1950s. Local preservationists rescued the building, and its reincarnation as a bed and breakfast restored life into this historic edifice. Retaining its original brick walls and interior wood beams, the Mill House exudes its own special charm. Guest accommodations include three rooms in the original mill and one in a new addition.

Marsha and Dave Frost, the affable hosts, thoroughly researched the business before opening their inn. They visited a variety of inns and incorporated the best features of each into the Mill House. Obviously at ease in their role as hosts, they know what it takes to make their guests feel welcome. Their comfortable, casual manner made us feel as if we were visiting old friends.

Common features throughout the immaculately clean inn include: private baths with fluffy towels, toiletries and nightlights; a choice of lighting options so that you can set the mood you prefer; a shopping bag to carry with you as you stroll the shopping district, and a dish of candies in each room. Marsha's creative handiwork includes glazed walls, which are hand-painted or stenciled with colorful floral designs. Her flair for decorating is evident throughout, especially her ability to embellish found objects and arrange them into an eye-pleasing mix.

The Garden Room is located in a rear addition with its own private entrance. It has wicker furniture, a unique picket-fence bed built by Dave, and an abundance of windows looking out over the river and canal. The bathroom contains a whirlpool.

The three rooms in the original building are floored with maple from a bowling alley. Each room contains a bowling pin, a whimsical tribute to its former use. Exposed brick walls, rough siding, and Marsha's flowers grace the walls, which have 7-foot windows. The bath contains a shower and has drinking glasses and outlets for appliances.

Our room, the spacious Edward Howard Room, contained a queen, single, and extra rollaway bed. An armoire for clothes and luggage and a dresser provide ample storage space. Sunflowers and cornflowers—handpainted by Marsha—brighten the room. Rugs are scattered on the floor and the windows are dressed in lace curtains and miniblinds.

The smallest room, The Jacob Kundert, has a double fourposter bed, a marble-topped dresser, and juvenile paintings hanging on the wall. Named after Jacob Kundert, an uncle of Dave's who operated a lock on the canal, this room is done in shades of blue. The foul line from a bowling lane is in the bathroom—but don't worry about a buzzer going off when you cross!

The Ruth Thomas room, located at the back of the house, has a queen-size brass and metal bed as well as a Jenny Lind twin bed. The walls are glazed peach and graced with hand-painted flowers. The windows offer a pleasant view of the canal and the garden.

The common room is tucked in the back of the house. Its sliding glass doors provide views of the river and access to the patio and garden. Furnished with a cushy loveseat and chair, as well as a table and chairs for evening refreshments, this comfortable room is the ideal place to peruse one of the books on local history or a magazine from the shelf. Or you can relax with a glass of sherry from the decanter on the buffet, which hides a TV and VCR for guests' use.

A hearty breakfast, which will keep the most ravenous cyclist energized, is served in the upstairs dining room in the Frosts' living quarters. Fruits, granola, baked bread, and a hot main dish are served with juice and a hot beverage of your choice. The Frosts have an enclosed storage place for your bikes and maps for additional routes on hand. They can advise you on restaurants and other activities in the area.

Biking from the Mill House
The terrain, ideal farmland that it is, is virtually flat; the only blips occur along the Maumee River between Waterville and Grand Rapids and should pose no problems to the casual cyclist. Water towers—obvious landmarks in these parts—dot the landscape and herald your arrival into the small towns along the route.

Liberty Center, the smallest of the towns along the route, offers an unexpected, trendy tearoom—a real treat for a break off the bike. A few other shops and restaurants huddle together in this one-block stretch of main street.

Waterville boasts a bigger water tower and a larger population; in fact, it's about to lose its village status. Another river town, its compact business district boasts a variety of shops and restaurants. The Columbian House restaurant comes complete with a ghost that supposedly haunts the ladies restroom. A short cycle out of town leads to Farnsworth Metropark, a perfect spot for a picnic or watching the river flow by.

Terrain: The flatness of the region makes this a fairly simple ride. The only ups and downs are between Waterville and Grand Rapids along River Road. Be forewarned that although the terrain poses few challenges, the winds can more than make up for it.

Road Conditions: Roads are all paved. Pay attention to gravel at some of the intersections. Some of the roads become very narrow.

Traffic: Except for the stretch along River Road, there is very little traffic. River Road is very busy during times when Grand Rapids hosts its renowned Apple Butter Festival. Use caution on the stretch of US 24, as this carries heavy traffic. This is just short jog, and there is a wide shoulder.

Mountain Biking Opportunities: Between Providence Park (just over the bridge and to the right) and Farnsworth in Waterville there is a tow path of about 9 miles that runs along the river; be sure that the river is not too high. The Turkeyfoot area of the Mary Jane Thurston State Park offers 6 miles of trails. The park is located off US 24 just beyond Texas, Ohio. Also nearby, starting in Liberty Center, is the Wabash Cannonball Trail, a converted rail-trail. The Maumee State Forest also provides opportunities for mountain biking.

Additional routes: David and Marsha have other route suggestions for those who would like to do additional riding.

Nearest Bike Shop
Cycleworks
248 South Main Street
Bowling Green, OH 43402
Phone: (419) 352-8578

Liberty Center Loop (23 miles)
This route follows the Maumee River at the beginning and then crosses into a flat agricultural area. Big barns, the Liberty Center tea room, Waterville, Otsego Park, and the Maumee River are some of the highpoints of this trip. A short out-and-back segment leads to Farnsworth Metropark, a good spot for lunch. Otsego Park provides a nice riverside spot to refresh and enjoy the scenery and wildlife. If you have the right type of bike, you could choose to ride the towpath along the river from Farnsworth Metropark back to Providence Park in Grand Rapids.

Cume	Turn	Street/Landmark
0.0	R	From Mill House, turn right onto **Front**
0.4	L	**W. 2nd**
7.7	R	**Rt. 109**
8.2	L	**Rt. 24**; *caution:* immediately get into right turn lane
8.3	R	**Rt. 109**
10.5	R	**Maple**
10.6	-	East St., on the left, goes to downtown and the tea room
13.3	L	**4A**
14.3	R	**County U**
18.1	S	Road veers to right a bit
19.1	R	**Manore Rd.**
21.1	L	**Manore Rd.** (yes, this is correct, the road has been realigned.)
21.9	L	**Ludwig**
22.2	R	**Grand Rapids**
22.5	S	**US 24** (*use caution*)
22.7	R	**Front**
23.0	R	Mill House

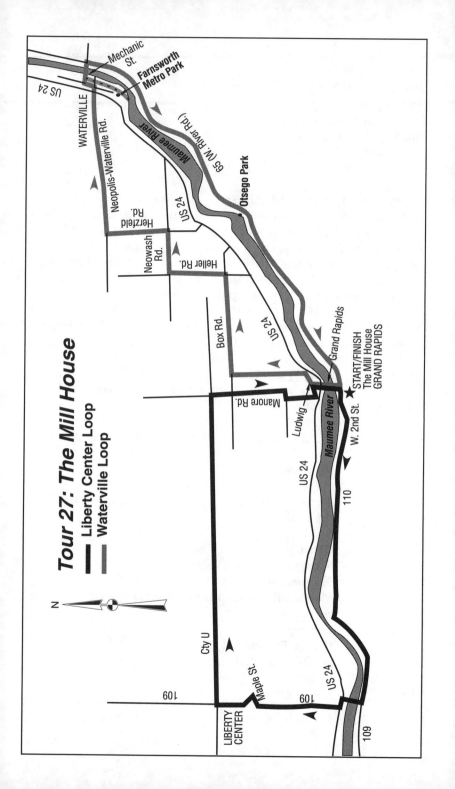

Tour 27: The Mill House

— Liberty Center Loop
▬ Waterville Loop

N

Mechanic St.
Farnsworth Metro Park
US 24
WATERVILLE
Neopolis-Waterville Rd.
Maumee River
65 (W. River Rd.)
Otsego Park
Herzfeld Rd.
US 24
Neowash Rd.
Heller Rd.
Box Rd.
US 24
Grand Rapids
Manore Rd.
Ludwig
START/FINISH
The Mill House
GRAND RAPIDS
W. 2nd St.
US 24
Maumee River
110
Cty U
Maple St.
LIBERTY CENTER
109
601
US 24
109

Waterville Loop (24.9 miles)
This ride starts by passing through farmland on back roads that lead to historic Waterville. Restaurants in town are available, but if you have a picnic lunch, a one-mile diversion to Farnsworth Metropark offers a perfect spot to enjoy your food and the Maumee River. If you have the right type of bike, you could follow the towpath from here to Providence Park in Grand Rapids.

Cume	Turn	Street/Landmark
0.0	**L**	**Front St.**
0.1	**L**	**Bridge St.**
0.3	**S**	Cross US 24—*caution!*
0.6	**S**	Railroad tracks—*caution!*
0.6	**R**	**Ludwig Rd.**
1.1	**S**	Railroad tracks—*caution!*
2.0	**R**	**Box Rd.**
5.6	**L**	**Heller Rd.**
7.1	**R**	**Neowash**
9.2	**L**	**Hertzfeld**
10.8	**R**	**Neapolis-Waterville**
13.1	**S**	*Caution* at intersection
13.2	**L**	Downtown Waterville
13.3	**R**	**Mechanic**
13.5	-	For detour to Farnsworth Metropark, turn right on S. River, go one mile, turn left on gravel path which leads to the park. Retrace route to return to Mechanic St.
13.9	**R**	**Rt. 65** (also called **West River Rd.**)
14.3	**BR**	Continue on **Rt. 65**
19.9	-	Otsego Park on the right has water and restrooms and a great view of the river.
24.9	**R**	Mill House

The Mill House, Grand Rapids, Ohio

Convention & Visitors Bureaus

Indiana

General Info:
www.state.in.us/tourism

Columbus Area Visitors Center (Always Inn)
506 Fifth Street, Columbus, IN
(812) 378-2622, outside Columbus: (800) 468-6564
e-mail: visitors@columbus.in.us
www.columbus.in.us

Nashville-Brown County Convention & Visitors Bureau (Always Inn)
Corner of Main & Van Buren Streets
P.O. Box 840
(812) 988-7303, (800) 753-3255
www.browncounty.com

Montgomery County Visitors and Convention Bureau
(Our Country Home)
218 East Pike Street
Crawfordsville, IN 47933
(765) 362-5200 (800) 866-3973
www.crawfordsville.org

Berne Chamber of Commerce (Schug House)
PO Box 85
Berne, IN 46711
(219) 589-8080
www.bernein.com

Peru/Miami County Chamber of Commerce (Cole House)
2½ North Broadway, Suite 202
Peru, IN 46970
(765) 472-1923
www.miamicochamber.com/tourism.htm

Richmond/Wayne County Convention & Visitors Bureau
(Historic Lantz House)
5701 National Road East
Richmond, IN 47374
(765) 935-8687, (800) 828-8414
www.visitrichmond.org

Marshall County Convention & Visitors Bureau (Culver House)
220 North Center
P.O. Box 669
Plymouth, Indiana 46563
(219) 936-9000, (800) 626-5353
www.blueberrycountry.org
Porter County Convention, Recreation & Visitors Commission
(Inn at Aberdeen)
800 Indian Boundary Road
Chesterton, IN 46304
(219) 926-2255, (800) 283-8687
www.casualcoast.com

Steuben County Tourism Bureau (Wild Winds)
207 South Wayne Street
Angola , IN 46703
(219) 665-5386, (800) LAKE-101
www.lakes101.org

Michigan
Michigan Travel Bureau
Lansing, MI
(888) 78-GREAT
www.michiganweb.com/travelbur.html

Oceana County Tourism Bureau (White Swan Inn)
100 State Street, PO Box 168
Hart, MI 49420
(231) 873-3982, (800) 874-3092

River County Tourism Council (Christmere House)
150 North Main Street
Sturgis, MI 49091
(800) 447-2821
www.rivercountry.com

Grayling Area Visitors Council (Borcher's)
213 North James Street
Grayling, MI 49738
(517) 348-2921, (800) 937-8837
www.grayling-mi.com/

Jackson Convention & Tourist Bureau (Coppys Inn)
6007 Ann Arbor Road
Jackson, MI 49201
(517) 764-4440, (800) 245-5282
www.jackson-mich.org/

Livingston County Visitors Bureau – (Bed of Roses)
207 North Michigan
Howell, MI 48844
(517) 548-1795
(517) 548-1795
www.htnews.com/lcvb/

Traverse City Convention & Visitors Bureau (Manitou Manor)
101 West Grandview Parkway
Traverse City, MI 49684
(800) TRAVERS
www.tcvisitor.com/

Saugatuck-Douglass Convention & Visitors Bureau (Will O'Glenn)
PO Box 28
Saugatuck, MI 49453
(616) 857-1701
www.saugatuck.com/

South Haven Convention & Visitors Bureau (Will O'Glenn)
415 Phoenix Street
South Haven, MI 49090
(616) 637-5252, (800) 764-2836
http://bythebigbluewater.com/

White Lake Area Convention and Visitors Bureau (White Swan)
124 W Hanson
Whitehall, MI 49461
(231) 893-4585
www.whitelake.org/

Ohio
General Info:
(800) BUCKEYE
www.ohiotourism.com/

Akron-Summit (Inn at Brandywine Falls)
77 East Mill Street
Akron, OH 44308
(330) 374-7560, (800) 245-4254
http://206.150.210.230/acasp/acpageL1New.asp?PageId=1

Convention & Visitors Bureau of Greater Cleveland
(Inn at Brandywine Falls)
50 Public Square
Suite 3100 Terminal Tower
Cleveland, OH 44113
(800) 321-1004
www.travelcleveland.com/

Greene County Convention & Visitors Bureau (Alpha House)
1221 Meadowbridge Drive, Suite A
Beavercreek, OH 45434
(937) 429-9100, (800) 733-9109
www.greenecountyohio.org/

Mansfield & Richland County Convention & Visitors Bureau
(Angel Woods)
124 North Main Street
Mansfield, OH 44902
(419) 525-1300, (800) 642-8282
www.mansfieldtourism.org/

Ottawa County Visitors Bureau (Ivy Guesthouse)
109 Madison Street
Port Clinton, OH 43452
(419) 734-4386, (800) 441-1271
www.lake-erie.com/

The Greater Toledo Convention & Visitors Bureau (Mill House)
401 Jefferson Avenue
Toledo, OH 43604-1067
(800) 243-4667
www.toledocvb.com/

Ross-Chillicothe Convention & Visitors Bureau
(The Greenhouse)
P.O. Box 353
Chillicothe, OH 45601
(740) 702-7677, (800) 413-4118
www.visithistory.com/

Coshocton County Chamber of Commerce (A Valley View Inn)
124 Chestnut Street
Coshocton, OH 43812
(740) 622-5411
www.utopianet.com/county/chamber.htm

Logan County Area Chamber of Commerce (Liberty House)
100 South Main Street
Bellefontaine, OH 43311
(937) 599-5121
www.logancountyohio.com/

Marietta / Washington County Convention & Visitors Bureau
(*Claire E*)
316 Third Street
Marietta, OH 45750
(740) 373-5178, (800) 288-2577
www.mariettaohio.org/

Selected Recipes

Sunday Morning Casserole
Always Inn
Nashville, IN

4 cups of bread, slightly toasted and cubed
2 cups of shredded cheddar cheese
10 eggs, slightly beaten
4 cups milk
1 tsp. dry mustard
1 tsp. salt
4 tsp. onion powder
1 tsp. oregano
Dash ground black pepper
1 lb. cooked, drained sausage
½ cup sliced fresh or canned mushrooms
½ cup chopped, peeled tomatoes (fresh or canned)

Butter 9"x13" ovenproof dish. Arrange bread on bottom, distributing evenly. Sprinkle with cheese. Beat together the next seven ingredients. Pour over bread and cheese. Layer sausage, mushrooms, and tomatoes on top. Cover and chill overnight. Bake at 325 degrees for 1 hour the next morning. For a different flavor, substitute the following ingredients: Swiss cheese, ham (leave out oregano), bacon and onion instead of tomatoes and sausage (leave out oregano).

Baked Cinnamon French Toast
Culver B&B
Culver, IN

12 slices cinnamon bread (raisin bread may also be used)
¼ c. butter or margarine, softened
9 eggs
2 cups whipping cream
1 cups sugar
4½ teaspoon vanilla extract

Line the bottom of a greased 13"x9" baking dish with six slices of bread. Butter the remaining 6 slices. Place with butter-side up over bread in pan. In a mixing bowl, beat eggs. Add milk, cream, sugar, and vanilla. Mix well. Pour over bread. Let stand for 15 minutes. Place the dish in a larger baking pan. Pour boiling water in larger pan to a depth of 1 inch. Bake, uncovered, at 375 for 40 minutes or until a knife inserted near the center comes out clean. Let stand for 10 minutes before serving.

Yield: 6 servings

Lemon Pancakes with Strawberry Butter
Historic Lantz House
Centerville, IN

½ cup whole-milk ricotta cheese (lite OK)
¼ cup small-curd cottage cheese
¼ cup butter, melted
¼ cup plus 1 tablespoon unsifted cake flour
3 egg yolks
3 egg whites
2 tablespoons sugar
juice of 2 lemons
pinch salt
¼ teaspoon cream of tartar

Place cheeses, butter, flour, egg yolks, sugar, lemon juice, and salt in food processor until smooth. Beat egg whites until foamy. Add cream of tartar. Beat until stiff. Fold whites into batter. Lightly butter hot griddle; pour into three-inch rounds. Cook until brown. Serve with strawberry butter.

Strawberry Butter: Mix ½ cup butter, softened, and ¼ cup strawberry preserves until well combined.

Aberdeen Pancakes
The Inn at Aberdeen
Valparaiso, IN

Line bottom of greased or non-stick pan with thawed brown and serve sausage. Mix your favorite pancake batter mix and pour over the sausage to a depth of ½" to 1."

Bake at 350 degrees for 45-60 minutes until golden on top. Add jam, caramel sauce, or maple syrup and put in the oven for a few more minutes. Remove from oven and let cool another few minutes before serving to aid slicing. This batter may be prepared the night before and refrigerated—just add a few more minutes of cooking time.

Lemon Curd
Bed of Roses B&B
Howell, MI

Lemon curd, also known as lemon cheese, is a very common English preserve. Use as a spread for sandwiches, toast, muffins, or scones.

Ingredients:
Grated peel of 3 lemons
Juice of 3 lemons (approximately 1 cup)
4 eggs, beaten
½ cup butter, cut into small pieces
2 cups sugar

In the top of a large double boiler, combine all the ingredients. Place over simmering water and stir until sugar is dissolved. Continue to cook, stirring occasionally, until thickened and smooth. Makes about 1 pint.

Pour into sterilized jars and cover. Allow to cool. Store in the refrigerator. Lemon curd doesn't keep indefinitely; make as much as you will use within a couple of weeks.

Petite Cinnamon Rolls

Borchers Bed & Breakfast
Grayling, MI

Roll out 1 package of crescent rolls into 4 rectangles. Sprinkle with cinnamon and approximately 2 tablespoons of sugar. Roll up rectangles and cut into four slices; place slices in a round baking pan or on a cookie sheet. Bake at 350 degrees for 25-30 minutes.

Frost with 1 cup of powdered sugar mixed with 2 tablespoons of milk (this will frost 2 or 3 cans of rolls).

Hash Brown Quiche

Coppys Inn
Grass Lake, MI

3 cups shredded hash browns
3 tablespoons butter or margarine, melted
3-4 drops Red Hot sauce
1 cup cheddar cheese, shredded
1 cup Monterey Jack cheese, shredded
3 eggs
¾ cup milk
Dash of Lowery's salt
1½ cups of a filling of your choice. Suggestions include sausage (cooked and drained), mushrooms, spinach, green or red peppers, or broccoli.

Pat potatoes into a 9-inch pie pan to form a crust. Drizzle melted butter over potatoes. Bake in 400-degree oven for 15 minutes to set the shell.

Prepare filling and arrange in shell. Dot with hot sauce and top with cheese.

Blend eggs, milk, and salt. Pour over filling in crust. Bake in a 350-degree oven for 45 minutes or until eggs are set.

Fresh Asparagus and Dill Frittata

Manitou Manor
Leland, MI

½ cup yellow cheese (shredded)
12 eggs, beaten
12 asparagus spears
salt and pepper to taste
½ teaspoon dried or fresh dill
1 tablespoon Bisquick (most important)
2 tablespoons sour cream
Optional items: red and green pepper, diced ham, onions, mushrooms

1.   Sauté veggies and herbs in butter.
2.   Beat eggs with sour cream and Bisquick.
3.   Salt and pepper to taste.
4.   Remove asparagus from pan.
5.   Pour egg mixture into remaining sautéed veggies.
6.   Cook covered, on low heat for 5-8 minutes.
7.   Uncover pan and arrange asparagus in pinwheel on top.
8.   Sprinkle with shredded cheese.
9.   Cover with lid and cook for 2-3 additional minutes.
10.   Slide whole frittata onto serving plate and cut into pie-shaped wedges.
11.   Serve while hot.

Munro House French Toast

Munro House
Jonesville, MI

1 loaf of unsliced bread with ends removed. Slice into 8 thick pieces.
6 eggs
¾ cup orange juice
¾ cup half and half or evaporated milk
2 tablespoons vanilla
¼ cup sugar

In large bowl, mix ingredients well. Dip each bread slice into mixture and place in shallow baking pan or dish. Pour remaining mixture over bread slices. Cover and let soak overnight in refrigerator. Grill bread slowly (250 degrees on electric griddle) until golden brown on both sides. Toast may be kept in a 150-degree oven for up to two hours in a foil-covered pan. Keep the corners of foil turned up to allow for steam escape.

Serve with warm apricot syrup.

Orange Apricot Syrup
2 cups orange marmalade
2 cups apricot preserves
¼ cups sugar
¼ cup orange juice

Combine all ingredients in saucepan and cook over low heat until warm.

Blueberry-Walnut Coffeecake
White Swan Inn
Whitehall, MI

1cup fresh blueberries
3 tablespoons brown sugar
1cup flour
1/3 cup sugar
½ teaspoon baking powder
¼ teaspoon baking soda
1/8 teaspoon salt
½ cup plain or vanilla non-fat yogurt
2 tablespoons margarine, melted
1 teaspoon vanilla
1 large egg
¼ cup chopped walnuts

Icing
¼ cup powdered sugar
1 teaspoon milk
¼ teaspoon vanilla

Combine berries and brown sugar in bowl, set aside.

Combine flour and dry ingredients in large bowl. Combine yogurt, margarine, vanilla, and egg in a small bowl. Add to flour mixture; stir until just moist. Spray 9" square pan with cooking spray. Spoon 2/3 batter into prepared baking pan. Top with berry mix. Spoon remaining batter over berries, top with walnuts. Bake at 350 degrees for 40 minutes or until wood toothpick inserted in center comes out clean. Cool 10 minutes on wire rack. Combine powdered sugar, milk, and vanilla. Drizzle over coffeecake.

Yield: 8 servings.

Irish Soda Bread (Spotted Dog)
Will O'Glenn Irish B&B
Glenn, MI

2½ cups all-purpose flour
1½ cups raisins
1 teaspoon baking soda
1 teaspoon double acting baking powder
5 tablespoons sugar
½ cup butter or margarine
1 cup buttermilk

In small bowl, pour boiling water over raisins; let stand 5 minutes. In large bowl, sift flour, soda, baking powder, and sugar. Cut in butter until mixture looks like coarse crumbs. Drain raisins, stir into flour mixture. Add buttermilk. Stir vigorously with fork.

Shape into ball. Place on greased 8-inch pie plate. Bake 15 minutes at 400°, lower heat to 375° and bake for 30 more minutes, or until knife comes out clean.

Dutch Babies
AngelWoods Hideaway
Lucas, OH

1/3 cup butter
4 eggs, slightly beaten
1 cup milk
1 cup flour
1 teaspoon granulated sugar
1/8 teaspoon nutmeg
2 tablespoon powdered sugar

Preheat oven to 425 degrees. Melt butter in two 9" glass pie pans. Mix eggs, milk, flour, granulated sugar, and nutmeg. Pour mixture into prepared pans. Bake for 20 minutes or until puffy. Sprinkle with powdered sugar during last few minutes.

Topping
2 cups sliced fresh fruit
½ cup firmly packed brown sugar
½ cup sour cream

Spoon fruit into center of pancake. Sprinkle with brown sugar. Top with sour cream.

Fruit Slush
A Valley View Inn
New Bedford, OH

2C   Sugar
3C   Boiling Water
12 oz. Frozen Orange Juice Concentrate
6-8   Bananas, sliced
20 oz. Can Pineapple, crushed
18 oz. Lemon-lime soda

Dissolve sugar in boiling water. Add orange juice. Slice bananas into mixture. Add can of pineapple. Add soda. The innkeepers at A Valley View Inn make this in a large plastic bucket and freeze it until needed. Makes 20-24 servings.

Swiss Breakfast Parfait
Alpha House
Alpha, OH

1 cup oatmeal (uncooked)
2 - 8 oz. containers of vanilla yogurt
1 - 8 oz. can of pineapple (undrained)
2 tablespoons sliced almonds
2 cups strawberries (sliced)

Combine oatmeal, yogurt, pineapple, and almonds. Mix well. Cover and refrigerate overnight. To serve: layer the oatmeal mixture with strawberries in 4 glasses. Garnish top with strawberries if desired. Serve chilled.

Quick Cheese Danish
The Ivy House
Marblehead, OH

2 cups biscuit mix
¼ cup butter or margarine softened
2 tablespoons sugar

Cut these together until crumbly. Stir in 2/3 cup milk. Beat 15 strokes by hand. Preheat oven to 450 degrees.

Spray cookie sheet. Drop by spoonfuls about 2" apart. Puddle of dough should not be more than ¼ cup. Make a well in dough puddle. Spread preserves on—raspberry is wonderful. Add a dollop of cream cheese mixture. Bake 10-15 minutes. Glaze. Remove to cooling racks as soon as removed from oven.

Cheese mixture
8 oz. cream cheese, softened
2 egg yolks
¼ cup sugar
Drop or two of yellow coloring
½ teaspoon of almond extract

Beat together. This has a long shelf life if kept cold in sealed container.

Glaze
½ cup Confectioners sugar
¼ teaspoon almond extract
1-2 tablespoons water

Mix well. Should be liquid enough to drizzle over pastries.

Cranberry Cake
The Mill House
Grand Rapids, OH

2 sticks butter (softened)
2 cups sugar
4 eggs
2 cups flour
½ teaspoon vanilla
1 teaspoon baking powder
1 pint berries (coated with ¾ cup flour) (blueberries are also good)
¾ cup flour for coating berries

Preheat oven to 325 degrees.

Grease and flour a tube pan.

Cream sugar and butter. Add eggs one at a time. Add remaining ingredients. Beat until smooth. Fold in berries. Bake for one hour and fifteen minutes.

Easy Cream Cheese Danish

The Cornerstone Inn
Archbold, OH

2 packages crescent rolls
1 egg, separated into yolk and white
2 - 8 oz. packages cream cheese
1 cup sugar

Spread out 1 package of crescent rolls on the bottom of a 9"x13" pan. Press seams together. Mix together cream cheese, sugar, and egg yolk. Spread on top of crescent roll in pan. Lay down second package of crescent rolls on top of the cream cheese mixture. Press seams together first. Whip egg white and spread on top. Sprinkle with a little sugar and cinnamon, if desired. Bake at 350 degrees for 30 minutes. Let cool before serving.

Fruited Oatmeal Soup

Inn at Brandywine Falls
Sagamore Hills, OH

4½ cups milk (2% is good, but skim will work)
2/3 cup rolled oats, quick-cooking or regular, but not instant
2/3 cup oat bran
Fruit of your choice—two pears, apples,* peaches, etc.—pared, cored, and chopped

Mix milk, oats, and bran in Pyrex bowl. Microwave, covered, on full power for 10 minutes. Remove and stir. Add fruit. Microwave at half power for 5 more minutes. Remove, stir.

If necessary, microwave at 30% power for 5 more minutes. Remove, stir, and keep hot over simmering water until served.

Serve with accompaniments of milk, brown sugar, granola, sour cream, or whatever else might appeal.

*Hard fruits, such as apples or dried fruits, such as apricots or dates, should be added at step 1.

Note: Other good fruit combinations are peaches cooked in the soup with fresh raspberries sprinkled on top; dried apricots (about 4 per person) which have been quartered and plumped by soaking overnight in boiling water to cover, whole green or red seedless grapes; apples with raisins.

Serves: 4 to 6